COLORING
GOD'S LOVE
FOR ME

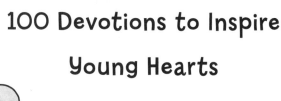

100 Devotions to Inspire

Young Hearts

By Janae Dueck

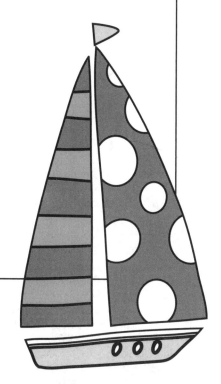

Coloring God's Love for Me: 100 Devotions to Inspire Young Hearts

Library of Congress Cataloging-in-Publication Data

Names: Dueck, Janae, author.
Title: Coloring God's love for me : 100 devotions to inspire young hearts / Janae Dueck.
Description: Nashville, Tennesse : Thomas Nelson, [2022] | Audience: Ages 6–9 | Summary: "This coloring book inspires kids and tweens to hold on to Bible promises of God's love, care, and protection. Each devotional includes a Scripture, a reflection on the verse using kid-friendly examples, and a coloring page that illustrates the promise "-- Provided by publisher.
Identifiers: LCCN 2021056414 | ISBN 9781400236343 (paperback)
Subjects: LCSH: Bible--Meditations--Juvenile literature. | Devotional literature--Juvenile literature. | Coloring books--Juvenile literature.
Classification: LCC BS491.5 .D84 2022 | DDC 242/.62--dc23/eng/20220111
LC record available at https://lccn.loc.gov/2021056414
ISBN 978-1-4002-3634-3

Images used under license from Shutterstock, iStock, and Creative Market.

Printed in the United States

22 23 24 25 26 CWM 10 9 8 7 6 5 4 3 2 1

Mfr: CWM / Robbinsville, NJ / June 22 / PO #12114813

CONTENTS

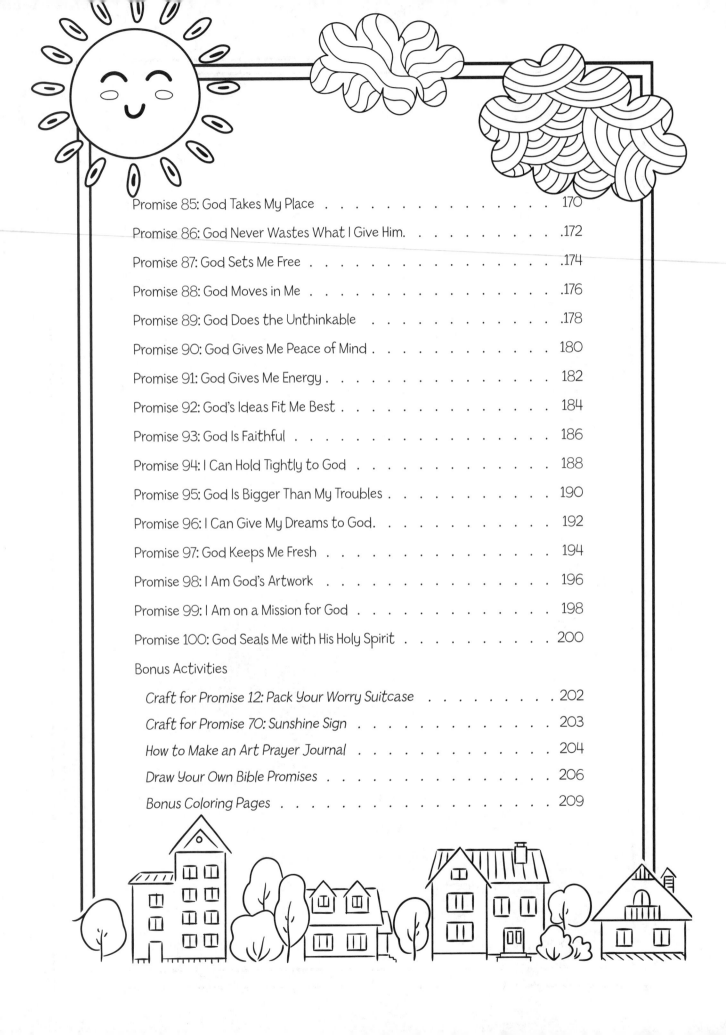

NOTE TO PARENTS

Pictures help us grasp big ideas. When your child pairs art with learning God's Word, the pictures are visual cues for remembering Scripture. Art accesses parts of the brain for learning and comprehension that reading does not activate. And just as journaling puts words to our feelings and experiences, creating with color and shape is a powerful way to communicate emotions, express thoughts, and bring about emotional healing. That's why art therapy is such a useful tool. Art therapy involves making art to manage and alleviate difficult feelings and to facilitate discussions of life experiences. It is especially helpful with children, who do not have the advanced language skills or self-awareness needed to identify and cope with how they feel.

This devotional invites your child to learn the big ideas of God's promises through playful pictures and fun analogies. I encourage you, as a parent or caregiver, to use these devotions to experience God's Word with your child in an interactive and playful way that creates meaningful discussion. Join your child in coloring the pictures. Draw and journal alongside them. Ask why your child drew something, or ask what they plan to draw. Keep the conversation going by adding more doodles to each promise or by making a craft. Think of this devotional as your child's sketchbook! Each page inspires new avenues to discover God's character. Learning His promises with pictures will bolster their understanding as they read the Bible and get to know the Creator of all beauty.

May each promise and picture inspire your and your child's hearts for years to come.

Janae Dueck

GOD KEEPS HIS PROMISES

And God said, "I am making an agreement between me and you and every living creature that is with you. . . . I am putting my rainbow in the clouds. . . . Floodwaters will never again destroy all life on the earth."

GENESIS 9:12–15

ROY G. BIV. No, that's not a famous person's name or an author you should know. It's the colors of the rainbow: red, orange, yellow, green, blue, indigo, and violet. Rainbows are a beautiful surprise. They stretch across the sky after a big storm to announce that the rain is over. Sunshine is coming again!

Did you know rainbows are a promise from God? Many years ago, God allowed it to rain for forty days. It rained so much that the whole earth flooded. A man named Noah believed God's warning about the flood and built a giant boat. God used Noah's boat to save a pair of each kind of animal and Noah's family. Once the flood was over, God made a rainbow. He told Noah that it was His promise. He would never flood the whole earth again. Even today, a rainbow is a reminder that God is still keeping His agreement.

What was the last promise you made? Or maybe someone made a promise to you. Did they keep that promise? People make agreements with each other all the time. But sometimes people forget about their agreements. God will never forget about His promises. And He has agreed to give you many things! God promises to love you, forgive you, protect you, and always be with you.

Next time you see a rainbow, remember God's big agreement with Noah. He is still honoring His promise—even though Noah has been gone for ages. That's just how God is. He keeps all His promises. And He'll keep the promises He makes to you!

PROMISE 2

I AM ON GOD'S TEAM

But we thank God! He gives us the victory through our Lord Jesus Christ.

1 CORINTHIANS 15:57

Imagine you just won a gold medal at the Olympics. You and your teammates stand on a podium. You can barely hear each other over the roar of the crowd. Goosebumps tickle your arms. Your heart races as someone slides a heavy medal over your head.

If you follow Jesus, you are a winner in a contest much bigger than the Olympics. When Jesus died on the cross, He won the contest with the devil over sin. Sins are the things you do that are wrong, like saying hurtful words or lying. Sin hurts God's heart and breaks your friendship with Him. The Bible says that the price of sin is death. But Jesus paid for sin with His own death on a cross. When you follow Him, He gives you the prize He won: a forever home in heaven with God.

To become an Olympian, you have to work really hard. Run faster. Train longer! Rest. And repeat. But to receive the prize of eternal life in heaven, all you have to do is join God's team. Jesus already did the winning work. So how do you suit up for God? Decide to let Him be your team leader, and ask Him to forgive your sins.

Now stand on the podium next to Jesus. Feel the medal slide over your head. Wear it proudly. With Jesus, you always win. You are on God's team!

GOD LEADS ME

"I am the Lord your God. I teach you to do what is good. I lead you in the way you should go."

ISAIAH 48:17

Have you ever been through a maze? You turned right, then left, then right. You backtracked at a dead end and tried again. But all you could see were walls. Perhaps you even needed help to find your way out. Or maybe you've tried to solve a maze on paper. This way? Erase. That way? Erase. It can take many tries to find the path out.

Life can feel like a maze. The pop quiz asks mostly about the lesson from the day you were home sick. Twist. A parent gets a new job, and you have to move. Turn. The doctor still doesn't know why you're feeling ill. Dead end. When unexpected things happen, you may question God. Does He care about what is happening? Has He left you alone in the maze?

God is with you in the maze. He is your leader who knows every turn. He knows exactly where you are. He knows where He wants you to go. In fact, He's handed you a map: the Bible. There are lots of helpful directions inside God's Word: Act like Jesus acted. Choose kindness. Stay away from people who get you in trouble.

Follow God's map. And when you can't see what's ahead, ask for help. God knows the best way through your maze. There is no maze too hard for Him to solve.

Complete the maze, and thank God for being your leader who knows where to turn.

GOD LIFTS ME HIGH

The Lord lifts up people who are in trouble.

PSALM 146:8

Imagine flying in a hot-air balloon. You climb into the giant basket. Then the ground slowly sinks away. What an adventure!

To make a balloon fly, a pilot uses a burner to heat the air in the balloon. The hot air weighs less than the cooler air outside, and the balloon rises off the ground. The balloon floats above rushing cars, scurrying people, and noisy machines. It lifts the people inside above all the noise into the quiet clouds.

Like hot-air balloons lift people over busy streets, God can lift you above your troubles. Are you worried about a test or tryout? Is your best friend in a different class this year? Or maybe your parents are arguing. These troubles can make you feel like a saggy, empty balloon. You need God to warm your spirit until you soar.

Next time a problem is keeping you down, talk to God about it. When you spend time with Him, His warmth will make you feel lighter. He will lift you out of the confusion around you. Your problem may still be there on the ground below. But you'll feel His quiet peace. Next, ask God for help. He might calm your mind during the test. He might show you a new student who needs a friend. He might ask you to remind your parents that He can lift them into His peace too. Or He might just remind you that He is flying your balloon.

Go to God with your troubles. He will lift you up high into His peace. With Him, you will rise!

As you color the hot-air balloons, tell God your troubles. Imagine rising over all the difficult things in your life and into the peaceful clouds.

GOD FILLS MY HEART

I pray that the God who gives hope will fill you with much joy and peace while you trust in him. Then your hope will overflow by the power of the Holy Spirit.

ROMANS 15:13

What is your favorite drink? Do you crave bubbly root beer? Is your go-to treat sweet chocolate milk? Or maybe you thirst for fresh lemonade. Whatever your choice, you want as much of that yummy drink as you can get. Maybe you've even filled a cup so high that the drink spilled over.

God wants to fill you up with His bubbly joy and fresh peace. When you spend time with God, it's as if you're handing Him an empty cup. God will pour His Holy Spirit into your heart. Are you anxious about a new school year? Did a grandparent get sick? Or is it just any old day? Give your cup to God by praying, reading your Bible, and worshiping. He will fill you up!

God will fill your cup to the very top—and then even more! Imagine that you could have all the root beer or chocolate milk or lemonade in the world. After a few cups, you wouldn't be able to drink anymore! And of course, your parents would never allow you to have that much sugar anyway. But you can never run out or have enough of God's tasty goodness. His Spirit will fill you up. And His joy and peace will spill out onto others.

Go ahead. Try it! Go to God and hold out your cup. Open your Bible. Tell Him about your day. Praise Him for your blessings. You'll never get too full.

Inside the glass, write or draw
things that bring you joy.

GOD PROTECTS ME FROM THE DEVIL'S TRICKS

But the Lord is faithful. He will give you strength and protect you from the Evil One.

2 THESSALONIANS 3:3

Have you ever been outside in a big storm? Black clouds cover the sun. Thunder shakes the sky. And wind tosses cold, large raindrops in every direction. The only way to stay dry in heavy rain is to wear a raincoat. Zip it up tight. The water and wind can't get in!

The devil likes to send storms into your life. Divorce, a lost pet, or a fight with a friend shake you like thunder. Negative thoughts soak you with doubt, fear, and anger. *I can't do that. What if that happens? I hate him.* The extra noise can make it hard to hear God.

Like a raincoat covering you from head to toe, God's truth in the Bible can protect you from the devil's stormy tricks. With God's Word covering you, you can stand strong in the middle of the noise. His truth will shield you from those cold, wet thoughts that pour down. Zip up your raincoat by memorizing Scripture. Here are a few verses to get you started.

- God will be with you always (Matthew 28:20).
- God has shown you His grace in giving you different gifts (1 Peter 4:10-11).
- Nothing can separate you from God's love (Romans 8:38).
- God will not let you be tempted more than you can handle (1 Corinthians 10:13).

This raincoat of new thoughts from God will keep you warm and dry. You don't have to fear the devil's storms. God's Word will protect you.

I AM STRONG IN GOD

"The person who trusts in the Lord . . . will be strong, like a tree planted near water."

JEREMIAH 17:7–8

Have you ever stood underneath a really tall tree? Its trunk is so wide that your arms wrap only partway around. Its branches crowd the trees next to it. Thick roots poke out of its sides. A riverbed sits nearby, giving the tree bucketloads of water.

God wants you to be as strong as a tree. Like a tree that grows by soaking up water through its roots, you can strengthen your faith by trusting God. Trust means believing what He says in the Bible. It means counting on Him to take care of you. And it means agreeing with God that you are in a good place in your life.

Soak up God's water by practicing ways of trusting Him:

- Ask for forgiveness when you do something the Bible says is wrong.
- Look for blessings everywhere.
- Remember that God is good and wants good things for you.
- Thank God for what you're learning at school.

Trusting God can be hard. But the more you stretch toward Him, the bigger your faith will grow. He is your water supply that will never run dry. He will make you strong.

GOD PULLS ME INTO ADVENTURE

I keep the Lord before me always. Because he is close by my side I will not be hurt. So I rejoice, and I am glad.

PSALM 16:8–9

Imagine balancing on two thin planks floating in the middle of a lake. You can't see how deep the water is. The shore is too far to reach by swimming. Sounds scary, right?

But what if those thin planks are water skis? You grip a rope pulled by a boat and soar across the waves. What a blast!

God wants your life to be a joyful adventure. And like a water-skiing rope, He will pull you into that adventure while also keeping you safe.

Are you in the middle of a deep challenge? Do you have a goal that you don't think you can reach? Maybe you volunteered to collect food cans for a local food pantry, but donations aren't coming. Don't give up! Grip the truth that God loves every person, and keep asking for donations. You'll make a difference and maybe make a new friend too. Or perhaps you want to play guitar, but your fingers can't hold down the strings. You can do it! Grasp onto the fact that God created music, and keep practicing. Maybe in a couple of years, you can join the worship band.

When you follow God, He gives you awesome opportunities. They might seem difficult. But hold tight to Him. Let Him pull you forward in His exciting plan. And enjoy the ride!

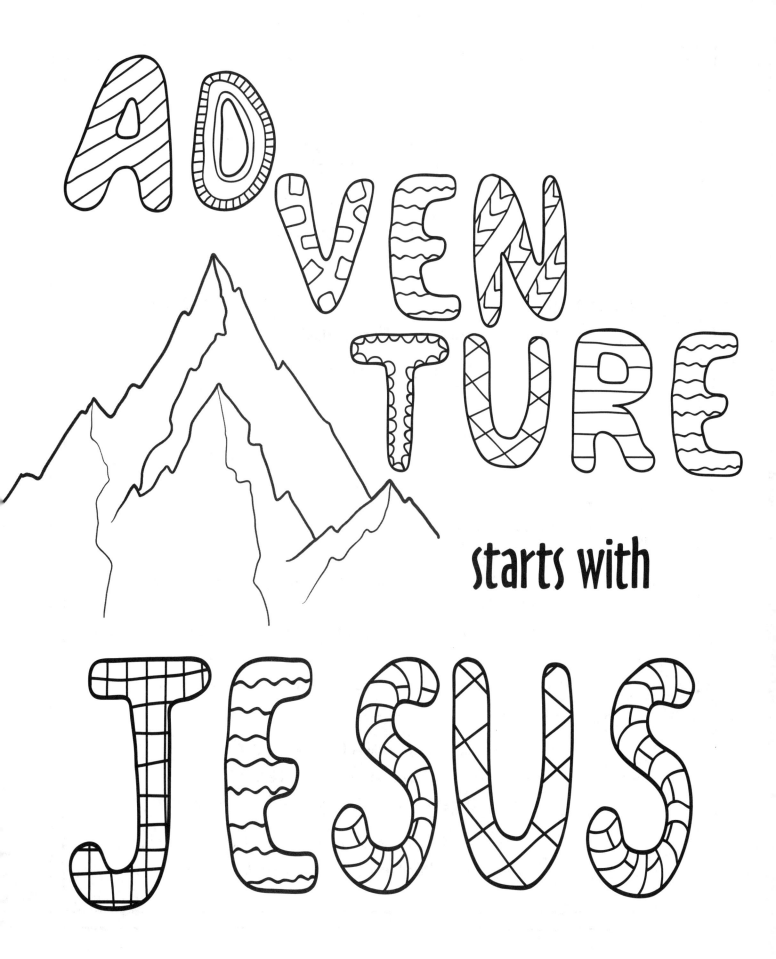

ADVENTURE starts with JESUS

I CAN DISCOVER WISDOM

Choose my teachings instead of silver. Choose knowledge rather than the finest gold. Wisdom is more precious than rubies. Nothing you want is equal to it.

PROVERBS 8:10–11

Have you ever found a cool rock? Miners dig for rocks deep in the ground. Sometimes they even find treasure like gemstones! Miners wear helmets with lights to see in the dark. Is that a diamond hiding in the dirt? Or just some coal?

God has left treasure for you to dig up too. These precious gems are the wisdom found in Scripture. When you live by God's truths, you are wise. Do you have a question about a verse you just read? Are you stumped on how God can forgive all your mistakes? Or did your friend ask you why you follow Jesus? Open your Bible and search for God's treasure. Ask an adult to help you find a verse that answers your question. Or find a passage that makes you happy or feel comforted. The more treasure you find, the more exciting it gets. When you dig through God's Word, you're sure to find something precious. These gems of wisdom are just a start:

- Peace comes through prayer (Philippians 4:6-7).
- People who take advice are wise (Proverbs 13:10).
- Forgive others because God forgives you (Ephesians 4:32).

Turn on your helmet light and dig down in the Bible. Before you know it, you'll find a wise word from God glittering beneath the dirt.

What question do you have for God?
Find a verse about it.

I wonder:

Bible verse:

GOD TALKS WITH ME

"Ask me and I will tell you remarkable secrets you do not know about things to come."

JEREMIAH 33:3 NLT

You just got home from a busy day of school and sports practice. So much has happened since this morning! So you climb up on a comfy chair with your mom, dad, aunt, or grandpa. With the fuzziest blanket wrapped around you both, you share about the substitute teacher and your friend's joke and the bully at lunch and making a volcano. Then they tell you about their coworker's new kittens and the rotten tuna sandwich they found. You cuddle and chat until a sibling rushes in to tell you it's time for dinner.

God wants to hear all about your day too! And He also wants to share things that are important to Him. So find a comfy spot and start a conversation. Be honest with Him. Share things that make you happy and things that make you sad. Tell Him some big news you just heard. Laugh about a funny joke you learned at school. Then sit quietly and listen to what He has to say. Read what He's already written in the Bible. And when you pray, give God time to answer. When you ask Him what to do, does your heart know what's right? Or maybe you feel calmer or happier. That's God speaking to you!

The moment you start talking to God, He is already listening. You have all His attention. And there is no time limit. Not even a call for dinner can end your conversation!

Keep telling God everything. And keep listening. He loves talking with you!

While you color, imagine climbing up onto God's lap and cuddling in. What do you want to tell Him today?

GOD MAKES LIFE SWEET

"The thing you should want most is God's kingdom and doing what God wants."

MATTHEW 6:33

What do you put on your ice cream sundae? A drizzle of chocolate fudge. A dash of rainbow sprinkles. A spoonful of whipped cream. Topped off with a bright red cherry! Once the ice cream is covered in goodness, you blend it all to make a swirly, colorful treat.

God wants your life to be as tasty as an ice cream sundae. When you put His kingdom first by mixing Him into every part of your day, He will cover you in His sweet love.

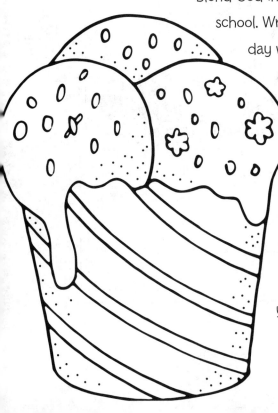

Blend God into your day however you like, in any order. Read your Bible before school. Write in your prayer journal before bed. Or tell Him your hopes for the day while you get cleaned up in the morning. Then sing a worship song after school. Each time you include God in your day, it's like taking a delicious bite of a loaded sundae.

Let God sweeten your day. What will your first topping be? Get creative. Draw a picture of a scripture, write a worship song, make a list of every silly thing you're thankful for (naked mole rats!). When you give God your attention. He'll give you energy much better than a sugar rush. And you won't crash an hour later!

The more you include God in your day, the sweeter life will taste. You can never have too many toppings.

GOD CARRIES MY WORRIES

Give all your worries to him, because he cares for you.

1 PETER 5:7

What's the longest trip you've been on? What did you pack? Don't forget your swimsuit. One underwear just won't do. You thought your game console could fit? As you add items, everything jumbles together. You might even have to sit on the suitcase to get it closed.

Packing a suitcase is only the first part of the job. Next, you have to lug that heavy bag to the car or across the airport. You probably need an adult to give you a hand.

Like a full suitcase, worries can be a big load. *Will I hit any shots in the game? Will I forget my lines in the play? What if I get hurt while my parents are away?* Your tummy aches. Your thoughts feel jumbled. Your mind is packed tight! But God says that you don't have to worry (Isaiah 41:10). In fact, He says to give your worries to Him.

Tell God your worries. As you share each problem or fear, imagine packing it in a suitcase. Zip the bag shut so nothing falls out! Then remember that God is strong enough to take care of you no matter what. Hand God your heavy load. And the next time a worry pops in your head, remember that God is carrying it for you.

Draw items that show your worries in the suitcase. Then imagine zipping it up and handing your heavy load to God.

GOD LIGHTS MY PATH

"I will make the darkness become light for them. And I will make the rough ground smooth."

ISAIAH 42:16

You're on a night walk. The only light on the path is the full moon. *Swoosh!* The wind blows behind you. *Hoo-hoo!* An owl calls from above. *Rustle!* Something scurries in the leaves. As you slowly take another step, your shoe almost kicks a large rock. But you see it just in time. The moonlight helps you walk safely on the path.

Like the moon on a dark night, God will brighten your path. Are you having a hard week? Is there a bully who won't stop calling you names? Did your friends plan a sleepover without you? These rough patches can make you feel like things around you are very dark. You can even feel dark inside.

When you go through difficult events, look to God. Sometimes He will help you see bumps so you can avoid them. He might remind you that being mean back to the bully will just get you in trouble. Other times, He will smooth out the path. Maybe the teacher lets you use the textbook during the quiz you were worried about.

Today, invite God into your dark places.

- Dear God, give me Your joy when I've had a hard day (John 16:24).
- Dear God, show me how to love someone who isn't kind to me (Matthew 5:44).
- Dear God, teach me to forgive my friends when they hurt my feelings (Ephesians 4:32).

When you walk behind God, He brightens your path. You can step forward with confidence. No tripping on rocks or roots. God's light shines much brighter than the moon!

I CAN HIDE IN GOD

God is our mighty fortress, always ready to help in times of trouble.

PSALM 46:1 CEV

Wind whistles outside. Snow blows sideways. But you know just what to do to stay cozy. First, you pull out two chairs. Then you drape a big sheet over the top. Grab a few pillows and some warm blankets. Then crawl inside your fort and snuggle in.

Like hiding in a blanket fort, you can crawl into God's arms for comfort. Is it your first day of school? Is a sibling sick? Or maybe you just want to curl up with some hot chocolate and be cozy. Go to God. He will shelter you. Find comfort in Him by praying, reading your Bible, and worshiping. You can even draw a picture of what God's fort might look like.

The fort that God provides is comfier than many pillows and blankets. So drag in your troubles and worries. Bring your warm feelings and good news. Sit with God and share these things with Him. His presence will comfort you like a cozy blanket.

Next time you're feeling troubled or in need of some extra comfort, curl up with God. Hide out with Him. He is your fort in times of trouble. He is always ready to help you.

He is

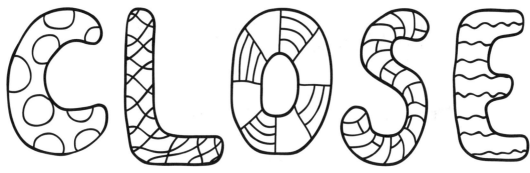

NAHUM 1:7 NLT

GOD KEEPS TRACK OF ME

You know when I sit down and when I get up. . . . You know well everything I do.

PSALM 139:2–3

What's the farthest you've run? One mile? Two? Marathon runners race for a whopping 26.2 miles in one day! These runners train for a long time to be able to run this far. And since the racecourse is so long, they wear tracking devices that record where they are. The device also tracks how long they've been running. And it tells how fast they've run each part of the race.

God keeps track of your location too. Like a tracking device, He knows everything you do. When you

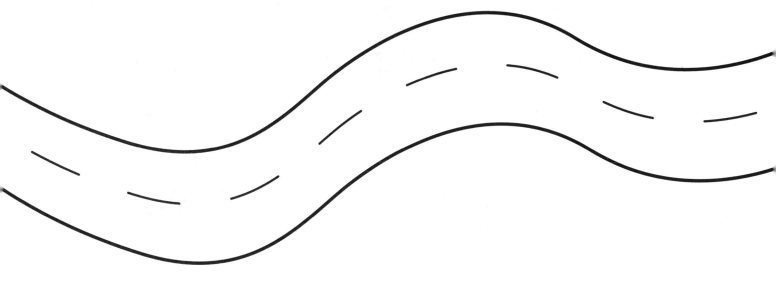

walk to school each morning, God follows you. As you make silly faces at your baby sister, God laughs along. At your grandparents' house, God sees each domino you play. Even when you don't go anywhere, God knows that too. You are always on His mind.

After a practice or race, the runner checks their tracker. It shows how fast they reached the finish line. Then the runner trains to beat that time for their next race. God will also help you do better when you check in with Him. He will encourage you that He made you to be smart and strong. He'll remind you that He is trustworthy. And He's always cheering you on.

God keeps track of each minute of your life. He loves to know what you're up to.

I CAN SOAR WITH GOD

**But the people who trust the Lord will become strong again.
They will be able to rise up as an eagle in the sky.**

ISAIAH 40:31

Eagles are rare birds. If you find one, make sure to take a picture! Their strong wings help them soar up to ten thousand feet above the ground. That's almost two miles high!

Like an eagle with powerful wings, you can fly high with God's strength. Were you asked to be the leader on your soccer team? Do you have an experiment to show at your school's science fair? Or maybe you have an idea for your Sunday school's service project! God gives you exciting opportunities. He empowers you when you take on new tasks. It's a chance for you to rise up with His strength and take on the challenge that's ahead!

After flying for a while, an eagle will swoop down to a nesting spot. Here it rests, lays eggs, and takes care of its chicks. Resting is an important part of getting stronger! As you tackle your challenge, remember to take quiet time with God. He might show you a verse that helps you be a better leader. He can give your brain a break from your science research so that you can think better when you work on it again. And He can give you the courage to tell your Sunday school teacher about your idea. Resting in God is like being in a nest. He will make your wings strong even when they aren't being used.

Today, think about the eagle and how powerful it is. Ask God to strengthen your wings like the mighty eagle's. Together, you and God can soar!

33

I CAN STAND ON GOD

"Everyone who hears these things I say and obeys them is like a wise man. The wise man built his house on a rock. . . . the house did not fall, because the house was built on rock."

MATTHEW 7:24–25

Pass a new neighborhood being built, and you will see large squares of concrete. These are the foundations for the new homes. The concrete base keeps a house steady. When rain and wind come, the house won't move. The concrete holds the weight of the house and protects those inside.

You can build your life on a foundation as strong as concrete. When you construct your life on God's truth, you will not lose faith when hard things come your way. Are you moving to a new home? Did you lose a home? Or did you lose a pet and your home feels different now? Things that disrupt where you live can make you feel unsteady. It can feel like a jackhammer is breaking up your foundation. It's not solid anymore. But even when life feels unsteady, you can be secure in God. Nothing can move Him. Make His truth, found in the Bible, your strong ground. Read a scripture verse and write it on a piece of paper so you can remember it as you move to a new place. Find a new favorite spot to read in your new neighborhood. Listen to your favorite worship song over and over again and dance in your kitchen. When you listen to God's voice, it is as if you're adding more concrete to your ground.

Do you feel unsteady? Pray to God. Read His Word. Praise Him. He will fill in any cracks with His truth. With His help, you can feel secure again. He is your solid foundation. Stand firm on Him.

GOD HEALS MY HEART

God, examine me and know my heart. Test me and know my thoughts.

PSALM 139:23

Have you ever had a checkup by a doctor? She might have you do funny things like stick out your tongue so she can look inside your mouth. Or she'll tap your kneecap and watch your leg jump. This can feel funny!

Just like doctors check your body, God checks your heart. He shows you sickness in your heart that only He can take care of. Sickness like pride, anger, fear, and shame can make you feel icky inside. These emotions can also make you act differently toward others and make them feel bad. But God wants to take care of your heart. He wants to examine you and heal every part.

God also tests your thoughts. He wants to know if your thoughts are like His thoughts. Are they hopeful? Are they true? If not, ask God to heal your thoughts.

Start with a prescription found in Scripture:

- Forgive someone who hurt you just like God has forgiven you. He will heal your heart from bitterness and anger (Ephesians 4:31-32).
- Give God your mistakes and remember that He is always faithful to forgive you. He will heal you from all the wrong you have done (1 John 1:9).
- Talk to God about a worry and let Him take it away from you. He will heal your mind with His peace (Philippians 4:6-7).

Next time you go to the doctor's office, remember that God takes care of you too. He heals your sick heart and brings health to your thoughts. Thank Him for being the best doctor around. His checkups help you feel your best.

GOD MAKES ME LAUGH

A happy heart is like good medicine. But a broken spirit drains your strength.

PROVERBS 17:22

What animals make you laugh? How about a clownfish? The word *clown* makes the fish's name funny to say. And what about those silly, bright orange and white stripes that look like clown clothes? Other fish look funny too. Some have big bulgy eyes. Some have large noses. Each one makes you smile!

God likes to make us laugh with the animals He created. He also likes to make us smile with other things. Do you have a sibling who makes you giggle? Is your teacher funny in class? Or maybe you're the jokester in your friend group. God loves humor. In fact, He uses it to cheer you up when you feel sad. God says a happy heart is good for your body and your mind.

When you are sad or disappointed, it's hard to be happy. And that's okay. Sometimes you need to feel sad for a time. But if you feel sad for a long time, you miss out on the good things God has for you. That's when God wants to give you a happy heart again. He might remind you of a worship song that will cheer you up. He might show you a cool scripture verse. Or He might use someone else to make you smile.

God loves to make you laugh. That's why He made the silly clownfish! And He wants to give you a happy heart when you think of His name.

GOD MOLDS ME

But Lord, you are our father. We are like clay, and you are the potter. Your hands made us all.

ISAIAH 64:8

Do you know how pottery is made? The potter takes a lump of clay and puts it on a spinning table called a *potter's wheel*. As the wheel spins, the potter presses the clay with wet hands. Slowly, the clay softens. It starts to take the shape of a bowl or vase or cup. The potter's hands move over the clay to form each part of the creation. Then the potter puts the piece in an oven called a *kiln* to bake and harden.

God is molding you like a potter molds clay on a wheel. He is shaping you to be more like Him. When you read His Word in the Bible, it's like He's softening you with water. When you pray to Him, He presses on your heart to form a vessel for His grace to fill. He is always working on you.

When you live in God's hands, He uses life's experiences to press you into His shape. If you get a new puppy, God might use your pet to teach you how to speak more gently. When a friend lies to you, God can use your wet tears to mold you into a more faithful friend yourself. As each experience spins by, He flattens your rough edges until they're as smooth as His righteousness.

Pottery takes a lot of patience. It takes time to shape a new creation. But turn by turn, day by day, God will form you into something beautiful and useful. Today, thank God for being your Potter. Ask Him to help you understand how He is shaping you. Trust the work of His hands. Now wait and see the cool creation He makes with you!

GOD CATCHES ME

When a man's steps follow the Lord, God is pleased with his ways. If he stumbles, he will not fall, because the Lord holds his hand.

PSALM 37:23–24

Have you ever jumped on a trampoline? You start with small jumps. Then bigger jumps. You and a friend hold hands and jump together. You jump so high that you hit the net and it sends you onto your stomach. What a landing!

Like a net around a trampoline, God catches you when you fall. When you lose control, you will stumble and make bad choices. But God will not let you fall too far. His net keeps you safe. Did you get upset and say a hurtful word to your best friend? Did you storm off instead of doing your chores like your parents asked? Maybe you told your teacher that you finished your homework, but you actually still had more to do.

God wants to help you get back on your feet. He is the friend holding your hand, jumping with you. He is happy when you make good choices. But He is also there to catch you when you go too far and make the wrong choice. He will forgive the hurtful words you say. He will teach you how to be honest and make things right. He will also help you learn to keep control and respond out of love and not from anger. Through it all, God's hand never lets go of yours.

Spend some time thanking God for catching you when you make a mistake. Hold tight to His hand, and ask Him to pick you up. Then get back to jumping!

GOD IS WORKING BEHIND THE SCENES

But Jesus said to them, "My Father never stops working. And so I work, too."
JOHN 5:17

It's your big day. You've been counting down the minutes until the show begins. You've practiced all your lines. And you've got your costume on. The director tells everyone to get in place. He has made sure the set and stage lights are ready. The curtains slowly draw back. The music starts to play. It's showtime!

Like the director of a play, God works behind the scenes. Even when you don't see it, He is putting things into place. Are you waiting to hear which teacher you have this year? Did you sign up for a sport but don't know yet which team you're placed on? Or are you having to be patient for something else? Waiting can be hard. It's like waiting for the curtains of a play to open. But God is working while you wait.

God will set the stage and ready the lights so that you can shine for Him. And even when things don't go your way, He works everything for your good. If you forget a line or stumble as you walk onto the stage, His play will still be a success. His glory shines through even the mishaps. And even before you see His work, enjoy the backstage while you wait. Here are some ways to practice waiting on God:

- Get dressed in your costume by putting on God's armor (Ephesians 6:10–17).
- Practice your lines by memorizing scripture.
- Do a soundcheck by singing your favorite worship song.

When you find yourself waiting, remember that God is working behind the scenes. He knows what's best for you. He is putting things in place. Trust that the important pieces of the set, lights, and other cast members will be where they need to be when the show starts.

I will WAIT for GOD'S NEXT ROLE for me.

GOD TAKES ME IN A NEW DIRECTION

God is being patient with you. He does not want anyone to be lost. He wants everyone to change his heart and life.

2 PETER 3:9

You turn on your boat's motor. Slowly, you move away from the dock. You turn the wheel. Rotate it to the left a little. Now to the right. A paddle called a *rudder* is connected to the wheel underneath the boat. As you steer, the rudder pushes the boat in the new direction. Now you're going fast in the open water. You turn the wheel, and the rudder steers the boat toward your destination and away from any obstacles.

Like a rudder moves a boat in a new direction, God nudges you away from sin and toward Himself. He presents you with the option to follow Him. When you do, He moves you toward something better. What obstacles do you need to move away from? Do you get angry when your parents remind you about your chores? Is it hard to share your scooter with your sibling? Or maybe you said you ate one cookie when you really ate two.

God wants to help you make good choices and steer away from sin. Without a rudder, a boat will keep going in the same direction. But God doesn't want you to continue to get angry, be selfish, or lie. He wants to change your life. He wants you to be honest and caring. By turning away from sin, God makes you into the person He created you to be. He turns on your motor. And He pushes you into the open water toward His new plan for your life. There are exciting things ahead!

Ask God to help you make the right choices. Let Him take you in new directions. He will turn your rudder. And He will keep changing your heart.

I AM SAFE WITH GOD

In the morning I will sing about your love. You are my protection, my place of safety in times of trouble.

PSALM 59:16

Camping is so much fun, but you have to watch out for the creepy crawlies! Before you climb into your tent, your flashlight searches for creatures that would love to spend the night with you. A spider scurries, and you slap it away. A curious squirrel chatters overhead. Something rustles in the leaves. Quick as a blink, you slip into the tent and zip it tight. No critters in here! The tent keeps you safe from snakes, spiders, and even sneaky squirrels.

Like a tent that keeps you safe from wildlife, God keeps you safe in times of trouble. Do you get nervous when you have to speak in front of others? Do you feel like there's nothing to be cheerful about? Maybe you feel misunderstood by a parent or teacher. Some feelings can come like a bite out of nowhere. The sting might last a while. But God can take care of these stinging feelings. He will be your safe place to rest.

No creepy crawlies can stay in God's presence. He will shoo these biting feelings away when you give them to Him. God will teach you to be brave. He will give you His joy. And He will help you be honest with your parent or teacher. Let God zip you up into His comfort and guard you from what's roaming outside. God doesn't want you to be bothered by these lurking feelings that try to creep in and stay the night.

When you go to God for safety, you can relax in Him. You can wake up the next morning and sing of His love. Open the zipper and climb out of the tent. Feel the sunshine on your face. All the creepy crawlies are now gone.

GOD GIVES ME A WAY OUT

But when you are tempted, God will also give you a way to escape that temptation. Then you will be able to stand it.

1 CORINTHIANS 10:13

It's just like any other school day. Your teacher is writing on the board. Suddenly, the fire alarm goes off. *Errr-errr-errr!* You smell smoke. The teacher leads you toward the nearest door. A bright red sign flashes above: Exit. *Whew!* You have a way out.

When you are tempted to sin, an alarm will go off in your mind. Maybe your sibling is bugging you, and a mean word grows in your mind like a smoke cloud. Or your homework was difficult, and you know you could copy your friend's answers. You won't hear a real alarm, of course. But you might feel a tightening in your stomach. You might feel a nudge in your heart telling you to stop. You might think, *Should I really do that?* The decision is yours. Do you stay in the dangerous smoke of temptation or find the exit?

God doesn't get mad when you think about doing something wrong. He sends an alarm because He loves you. And for every temptation, He provides a way out. There is always a choice! Listen to God's alarm. The next time you feel tempted, pray. Ask God to help you walk out of the bad situation. God might help you say something kind to your sibling. Or He may tell you to play by yourself for a while until you cool off.

The next time you feel an alarm, remember it comes from God. He is with you. He leads you to the exit and away from the smoke of sin.

I have taken YOUR WORDS to HEART so I would NOT SIN against You.

~ PSALM 119:11 ~

GOD SATISFIES ME

When I wake up, I will see your likeness and be satisfied.

PSALM 17:15

What's your favorite dessert? How about a piece of leftover cake? The creamy frosting is too good to resist. You've been craving a slice since the morning. Yum!

Like enjoying a dessert you've been craving, you can feel happy and full in God's presence. Think of how you feel inside when you're around your parent or a best friend. God will make you feel complete and happy when you spend time with Him too. When you eat cake, you don't think about other treats. You might also like popcorn and Popsicles and Pop-Tarts. But with a sweet slice in front of you, you enjoy the soft cake and sweet frosting. In the same way, you can be satisfied with God and not focus on other things you'd like to have.

And unlike a dessert, you can enjoy God right away. You don't have to eat your veggies first! Right when you wake up, God is excited to see you. Enjoy His satisfying presence by reading your Bible and praying. Ask Him to help with your needs. Tell Him about your wishes and dreams. Do you hope to get a part in the play? Do you want a new gaming system for Christmas? Are you disappointed that the cool kids don't know your name? Tell God. Ask Him to help you be satisfied with all He gives you. The more you talk to Him, the less important those other things will seem. Nothing else can compare to spending time with Him.

You might crave one thing. You may wish for something you don't have. But God is all you truly need. Go to Him and savor His delicious love. He will make you feel complete in Him.

I CAN HELP BUILD GOD'S KINGDOM

We are workers together for God.

1 CORINTHIANS 3:9

What happens at a construction site? Workers use all kinds of tools and trucks to build. A crane lifts beams into place. A digger breaks up rubble and moves it out of the way. A saw cuts wood. And a bulldozer moves mountains of dirt! It takes an army of workers to construct a new building.

Like workers at a construction site, we are workers for God. He gives each of His children special jobs to build good things. Your teacher might ask you to read to a younger kid. Or your parent wants you to cook dinner once a week. Or maybe your pastor asks you to come up with an idea for a service project. Sometimes you're given big responsibilities. And they can feel like a lot of work. But remember that you are working for God. You can help build His kingdom. You can love others and tell them about the special work He has given you. You're on God's construction site called earth.

When you do God's work, He will lift you to Him. He will break away the lies that say you aren't old enough or smart enough to do His work. He will cut away past sin and move piles of shame that have been sitting for a long time.

You are one of God's workers. Join His construction crew and work together with others to build His kingdom on earth. So what are you waiting for? Start the bulldozer.

PROMISE 28

GOD'S LOVE STICKS

Nothing can separate us from the love God has for us.

ROMANS 8:38

What is the coolest craft you've ever made? Did you use a lot of glue? Maybe you made a cardboard house with tons of rooms. Or you glued together a thousand toothpicks to build a giant pyramid. By the end of it, your hands may have been glued together.

Like glue holds pieces of a craft project together, God sticks to you. Nothing can separate you from His love. It cannot be ripped away. God's love is as strong as superglue!

Sometimes you feel ripped apart from other people. Did you get in a fight with your best friend? Or maybe you got angry at your parents and refused to come to dinner when they asked you to. It can take a lot of work to put relationships back together when people get separated.

But no matter how much you fight God or what hurtful words you say to Him, His love sticks to you. He will never say mean things back to you. He will never think mean things about you either. He loves you no matter what. Nothing is strong enough to separate you from His super-sticky love. You and God are glued together!

Read Romans 8:38 next time you need to be reminded of God's love. Read it twice out loud if you have to! Thank God for how His love is sure. It will not tear or fall apart. It's stronger than any glue. He will hold every part of you to Him.

I have loved you with an

EVER
LAST
ING

Love

JEREMIAH 31:3 NIV

GOD'S LOVE GOES ON AND ON

And I pray that you and all God's holy people will have the power to understand the greatness of Christ's love. I pray that you can understand how wide and how long and how high and how deep that love is.

EPHESIANS 3:18

Chipmunks burrow tunnels in the ground. The tunnels can go three feet deep and reach up to thirty feet in length! In the center of the tunnels, a chipmunk digs a nest. Chipmunks also stash nuts and seeds in other holes along the tunnels to eat during wintertime. And they dig extra tunnels up to the surface for more entrances.

Like an underground tunnel system, God's love for you goes in all directions. It goes beneath you and around you. It is there even when you don't see it. You can experience God's love in many ways. Maybe a Bible story inspired you to draw a picture. Maybe you learned a worship song on your guitar. Or you told a friend about a time God answered your prayer. You burrowed into His love.

Or perhaps you haven't noticed God's love in a long time. Ask God to take you down a new tunnel of His affection. Then read the Bible. Make a list of blessings. Take a walk. As you spend time with Him, you'll find a whole tunnel system of love. He's stored up many nuts and seeds of care for you!

Here are some scriptures to burrow into that will remind you of God's deep love:

- God's love continues forever (Psalm 136:26).
- God's love never changes (Isaiah 54:10).
- God pours His love into my heart (Romans 5:5).

God's love is like an endless system of tunnels. It runs wide and long and high and deep. It goes on and on! And there are many entrances. All you have to do is find one.

GOD MAKES IT POSSIBLE

Jesus looked at them and said, "For men this is impossible. But for God all things are possible."

MATTHEW 19:26

Imagine that you come to the edge of a cliff. Beneath you is a deep canyon. Rushing water runs through it far below. How will you get to the other side? Then you notice a bridge not far off. You tromp across its sturdy floor.

Sometimes you face canyon-sized leaps in life. Getting to the other side of your problem or reaching your goal feels impossible. But God can build a bridge to the other side. Do you have lines to memorize for a school play? Do you have to make friends in a new neighborhood? Or maybe you're deciding between sitting with a new student at lunch or studying for a spelling test. Talk to God. He will give you a way forward.

When you put your faith in God, His power becomes your bridge. He might show you a trick to help you memorize your lines. He might give you courage to knock on your neighbor's door to introduce yourself. Or He might remind you that being kind is more important than getting good grades. Give God the situations that feel impossible or challenging. Ask Him to show you possibilities. Trust the bridge He builds in front of you. Even if it isn't what you expected, know that God is working to help you.

God will help you cross over big challenges. He will provide a way. Then you'll look back at how far you've come and thank Him for never leaving your side.

What feels impossible to you today? Write about it in the lines below. Then thank God that He will help you across.

_____

_____

_____

_____

GOD TRAVELS WITH ME

If I rise with the sun in the east, and settle in the west beyond the sea, even there you would guide me. With your right hand you would hold me.

PSALM 139:9–10

The van bumps out of the parking lot. Your parents wave goodbye as you settle your overnight bag between your feet. You're on your way to camp! There will be games, swimming, a campfire, and new friends. But no parents, no familiar bed, and no Saturday morning pancakes.

Even when you travel somewhere new, God goes with you. He is your travel buddy. He will never leave your side. Have you gone to overnight camp? Or maybe you've spent the weekend at a friend's house while your parents were out of town. Or you went on a trip with a relative. Leaving home without your family can be so exciting—and scary! But God says not to be afraid. He will go with you to these new places. Even if you fly east all the way to Africa, west to Hawaii, north to the Arctic Circle, or south to Brazil, God goes with you.

Traveling with God is like getting to take your best friend with you everywhere you go. Except that He will never leave. Not even when it's time to return home. So next time you go on a trip, remember that God is going with you.

Take some time to thank God for being your travel buddy. Wherever you go, He is there too.

GOD CLEANS UP MY MESS

He lifted me out of the pit of destruction, out of the sticky mud. He stood me on a rock. He made my feet steady.

PSALM 40:2

It has rained for an entire week. Puddles are everywhere. Time to put on those rain boots! Go find the biggest puddle to jump in. Take a leap and watch the water splash everywhere. Feel the oozing mud between your fingers.

It's fun to be muddy at first. But then it starts to feel gross. That's when it's bath time!

Sin is a little like a great big sloshy mud puddle. It can feel good in the moment. That's why it's easy to get stuck and keep doing bad things over and over again. But after a while, sin starts to feel gross.

God knew our sin would hurt us. He knew it would start to feel sticky like mud between our fingers. So God gave His Son Jesus to clean our sins. When you ask God to forgive you for doing something wrong, He will take you out of your dirty sin. Then He will stand you up on the solid rock of His forgiveness. From head to toe, God will scrub away all the muddy mess of sin. Your feet will no longer feel stuck. And no trace of your sin will be left. Not even a drop between your fingers. You'll be as fresh as when you get out of a bath!

GOD PUTS ME TOGETHER

God began doing a good work in you. And he will continue it until it is finished when Jesus Christ comes again.

PHILIPPIANS 1:6

Puzzles are a fun challenge. This piece goes there. That one belongs there. Before you know it, you'll see a hidden picture forming! And once there's already some pieces filled in, it's easier to place the others.

God has a place for all the pieces of your life. Each opportunity to be more like Him is like a new piece added to His puzzle. When you keep your temper, God places another piece of patience. When you thank God for a blessing, He adds a piece of gratitude. Some pieces will fall into place easily. Some pieces will feel more out of place. But piece by piece, God is putting you together to become more like Him.

Ask yourself what feels out of place. Are you the only child in your family? Does your family look different than other families? Do you have an interest that none of your friends have? Tell God that you trust the good work He is doing in you. He has great plans for your life. God placed you in your family for a reason. And He gave you that interest for something special.

God knows the best order for putting your pieces together. Even though it takes a long time and a lot of patience, He will finish His good work in you. One puzzle piece at a time, He is making you into something spectacular.

Draw parts of your life and your personality in the puzzle pieces. Thank God for these pieces. Tell Him that you trust what He's doing with them.

GOD'S INSTRUCTIONS ARE GOOD

Lord, you do what is right. And your laws are fair. The rules
you commanded are right and completely trustworthy.

PSALM 119:137–138

Twister is a game played with your whole body. First, take off your shoes so you don't squish other people's toes. Then spin. Everyone does the same action at once. Right foot to green. Left hand to red. But watch out! The next spin could send your right hand in the opposite direction. Soon you'll be twisted up! The rules of the game make it fun and wacky.

Like rules keep a game fair and fun, God's guidelines make life better. His rules aren't just a list of do's and don'ts. He gives you instructions so you can live a fair and fun life. For example, God wants you to be honest. This rule keeps you from getting twisted up with lies. He asks you to be kind to everyone. Following this rule means you can worship Him with all kinds of people!

In the game of Twister, if you fall, you're out. But with God's good instructions, you're never out. You can always start again when you make a mistake. Even if life spins you in a wacky direction, God will help you get straight again. If you fall, He will pick you right back up.

Remember God wants you to live your best life. His instructions will help you do that. But you don't need to keep a checklist of His rules. Instead, focus on Him. When you love God with all your heart, following His good instructions comes naturally. So keep His directions in the Bible close and get ready to play. When you follow God's instructions, your life will be fun and wacky.

YOUR RULES

give me

GOOD ADVICE

~ PSALM 119:24 ~

GOD KEEPS ME ON COURSE

I press on to reach the end of the race and receive the heavenly prize for which God, through Christ Jesus, is calling us.

PHILIPPIANS 3:14 NLT

Racecars can drive over 200 miles per hour. So racecar drivers have to be really careful. They turn hard when the course turns. They dodge a wheel that fell off another car. They swerve around a wreck. They ignore the crowd cheering as they race to the finish line.

God has placed you on a racecourse. He wants you to speed toward Him. But there are obstacles that can slow you down. Fear, doubt, sadness, and sin itself can take your attention away from God and cause a wreck. For example, if you're too afraid to speak up when a friend does something mean, it's like your car hit a loose wheel. You need to stop and repair your heart with the Bible's teachings on courage and boldness. Then get back on course in the direction God wants you to go. Some obstacles are so big that they can feel like a car wreck. Like getting in a fight with your parents. Or when someone hurts your feelings.

But God can help you continue the race. He will help you navigate around obstacles and distractions. And He can fix your car and get you back on course when you get in a wreck. God might help you say sorry to your parents. Or He might show you how to forgive someone who hurt you. He will repair your heart. Keep driving after Him toward the finish line of heaven.

Tell God about the obstacles you're facing. He will help you safely pass them and keep your focus on Him. He will keep you on course.

GOD MAKES ME BRAVE

**Evil people run even though no one is chasing them.
But good people are as brave as a lion.**

PROVERBS 28:1

What does a lion's roar sound like? Can you make that sound? Open your mouth wide. Now *ROAR!* Imagine that you're a lion cub. You are brave. You will stand up to any danger that comes near your den.

You can roar loud and fierce too—and not just when you're pretending to be a lion. You roar by being brave. Perhaps you are going on a plane and you feel anxious to fly. Or your teacher asked you to present in front of the whole class. Or maybe it is your first volleyball game or swim meet. You've practiced for weeks, but the nervous feelings won't go away. Your roar doesn't seem big enough. But like a lion cub, you can call on your fierce Papa. Your heavenly Father will stand in front of you. His powerful roar is bigger than any fear or danger. And with Him nearby, your roar will seem louder and mightier.

When a scary situation feels too big, call on God. He will help you be brave. With God, no fear can chase you away!

Here are some ways to roar your fear away:

- Tell God about your scary situation, and ask Him for courage.
- Read God's Word out loud, and ask Him for peace.
- Pray with an adult about your fear, and face it together.

The more you let God's voice in, the mightier your roar will be. He will make you brave. So make your roar loud. Show your teeth. And remember that nothing can chase you and God away.

I CAN FEEL THE WARMTH OF GOD'S PRESENCE

The Lord replied, "My Presence will go with you, and I will give you rest."

EXODUS 33:14 NIV

Imagine that it is wintertime. You are home for a snow day. After playing outside, you can barely feel your fingers. They are as cold as ice! Coming inside, you discover a fire crackling in the fireplace. You sit close to it and shut your eyes. The heat of the glowing embers thaws out your whole body. The warmth feels amazing!

God's presence also wraps you in warmth. His Holy Spirit is like a fireplace that is always on. You can sit close to Him and feel His presence crackling inside you. Do you ever find yourself thinking cold thoughts? Maybe you wish to be the first one picked for the basketball team. Or you are glad when a bully gets their feelings hurt. These thoughts don't come from God's love. But like a fireplace that draws you in from the outside cold, God's presence draws you back to the warmth of His Spirit. He will melt your cold heart and show you how to love others and put them first.

God promises to draw you into the warming love of His presence. When you have cold thoughts, write them in a journal and ask God to warm them. His embers will thaw out your icy thoughts by replacing them with His cozy truth.

Thank God for giving you His presence and for surrounding you with His warmth. Go to His fireplace when your thoughts feel cold. Let God thaw you out, all the way through.

GOD HELPS ME SEE

I tried to understand all this. But it was too hard for me to see until I went to the Temple of God.

PSALM 73:16–17

Have you ever been to the eye doctor? The doctor puts different lenses in front of your eyes. Then you read the letters on the wall. Some letters are big and easy to see. Some are small and hard to see. You might find out that wearing glasses helps you see things more clearly. Or you might not need glasses because you already see fine. Either way, it's good to check!

And just like the eye doctor, God also helps you see things clearly. You might avoid a kid who annoys you because He asks a lot of questions. You may wish to be friends with a kid who wears cool clothes. Or you might talk badly about a kid who says mean things. Sometimes, you don't know why a person acts a certain way. Or you see someone differently because of how they look. The world can feel confusing and blurry.

But God will help you see through His eyes. He views everyone through a lens of love. He loves the kid with old clothes just as much as He loves the kid who wears the cool brands. And He wants to have a relationship with the girl who makes fun of others—just like He wants to have a relationship with you. God wants to help you understand the world the right way—through His way of love.

Like the eye doctor helps you see clearly, God helps you see the world through His lens. When you view the world with God's perspective, you will understand how to live out His love and truth.

GOD KEEPS ME AFLOAT

Now this is what the Lord says . . . "Don't be afraid, because I have saved you. I have called you by name, and you are mine. When you pass through the waters, I will be with you. When you cross rivers, you will not drown."

ISAIAH 43:1–2

Have you ever been to a waterpark? Some waterparks have a lazy river. You lie in a comfy inner tube and float down the river. The moving water pushes you forward. If you try to stop, the people floating behind you will press against you. It is impossible to swim upstream! But as long as you sit on your inner tube, you stay afloat and enjoy the ride.

Like sitting on an inner tube in a lazy river, you can stay afloat on God during difficult life events. Did your sibling accidently ruin your big school project? Did you lose in a karate tournament? Or maybe you have to retake a test at school. These things can feel like a water current pushing you down. You might feel like you've lost control. But God keeps you afloat. Hold tightly to Him like you would to the handles of an inner tube. He will not let you float away. Hold onto God by reading His Word or by thanking Him for a blessing in your day.

Because you belong to God, He keeps your head above deep difficulties. He holds you up when life tries to push you down. Next time you feel the press of a difficult event, talk to God about it. He might give you a scripture verse to comfort you. Or He might put it on your heart to give a scripture verse to someone else who feels the pushing current too. You can stay afloat together.

Let God support you. He will keep you afloat when difficult things come. When you pass through deep waters, you and God can float with ease.

Connect the dots to complete the picture, then color it. As you work, tell God about something that is pushing you down.

GOD IS PREPARING ME FOR HIS WORK

In Christ Jesus, God made us to do good works, which God planned in advance for us to live our lives doing.

EPHESIANS 2:10 NCV

Have you ever made chocolate chip cookies? After mixing the ingredients, you place scoops of dough on a baking sheet. The baking sheet was built just right for making cookies. Its flat surface bakes the cookies evenly. And it was formed out of aluminum to withstand heat from the oven.

Like a baking sheet that makes the perfect cookies, you were made by God to do His good work. In fact, He makes sure that you're ready for the tasks He has planned for you. Were you asked to help your parents organize a meal for the church? Were you assigned a new school project to write a fictional story? Maybe you have to be brave with a classmate who asked why you believe in Jesus. God has thought ahead. He might be giving you these jobs to get you ready for something even more important.

God might give you special skills in cooking so you can make meals for a family who needs food. He might help you start a creative writing club so He can introduce you to a new friend who needs to hear about Him. Or He might make you a strong public speaker so you can speak out for Him. Like a cookie sheet is designed to bake cookies, you were designed to bring God glory in your own special way. He has big plans for you.

Doing God's work isn't always easy though. You will have challenges that feel like a hot oven! But God made you out of tough material to get through hard times.

Like cookies coming out of the oven, you can look forward to good things when you do the work that God designed you for.

GOD GIVES ME NEW ADVENTURES

Look at the new thing I am going to do. It is already happening. Don't you see it? I will make a road in the desert. I will make rivers in the dry land.

ISAIAH 43:19

You pedal your bike through your neighborhood. You pass by the same blue house. The same maple tree. And the same old barking dog on the corner. But then you notice a dirt road running along your neighbor's garden. *How did you miss it before?* You pedal down the new path with excitement. You are on an adventure!

Like exploring a new road, you can go on adventures with God. Sometimes your days can feel all the same. The same walk to school. The same cafeteria meal for lunch. Or maybe the same argument between you and your sibling. Things around you just don't change.

God wants you to look for new roads to explore with Him. Is there a kid who sits alone on the bus on your way to school? Invite him to sit with you. You might discover God has an awesome new friend for you. Or He might give your family the opportunity to go on a mission trip. You might learn a lot from the different people you meet and the new culture and language. Or maybe an elderly neighbor needs help in their yard. It sounds like a lot of work, but you might discover that your neighbor tells the funniest jokes or can teach you to play chess! You never know where God's new road will take you.

Ask God to take you on an adventure. Turn down a new road with Him. He wants to surprise you. It's time to pedal to new places!

GOD THROWS MY SIN FAR AWAY

Lord, you will have mercy on us again. You will conquer our sins. You will throw away all our sins into the deepest sea.

MICAH 7:19

You stand at the edge of the ocean. You grip a stick as you shift your shoulder backward. Then you swing your arm and toss the stick as far as you can. It splashes into the waves. You watch as the current carries it away.

Like someone who tosses a stick into the ocean, God wants to throw your sins far away from you. When you ask for His forgiveness, it's like He tosses your wrongs into the deepest ocean. Your sins get lost forever in the deep sea of His mercy and grace.

But sometimes you hold onto a sin. You keep remembering what you did. You keep feeling bad about it. It's like you're holding onto a rough stick that pokes your hand. But God doesn't want you to hold onto your sin. He wants you to throw it far away. Let Him make it disappear.

God will forgive you for each wrong you make. All you have to do is ask Him! His forgiveness is always waiting for you. When you make a mistake, take your sin to the edge of God's sea of forgiveness. Then throw!

God will toss your sins far away. He won't think about your wrong choices again (Jeremiah 31:34). So you shouldn't think about them either. The stick God throws will not float back. When He forgives, He forgives forever.

GOD RIDES WITH ME

Trust the Lord with all your heart. Don't depend on your own understanding. Remember the Lord in everything you do. And he will give you success.

PROVERBS 3:5–6

You climb into the roller-coaster car and buckle up. The track pulls the car forward. *Clickity-click-click.* You go up . . . up . . . up . . . up. Right as you get to the top, your seat tilts down. In front of you is the steepest drop of your life! Your stomach seems to drop too. You throw your hands up as the roller coaster rushes down, around, up, and then down again. Your body leans in every direction. It's a wild ride!

Life can feel like a roller coaster. When unexpected drops happen, you might feel pulled in different directions. Your stomach may even drop when you don't know the future. Did you get a bad grade? Is your friend having surgery? Or did a doctor tell you news you weren't expecting? No matter how steep or fast the dip, trust God. He is your safety belt.

When you go through trouble, it's easy to try to make things better by yourself. But that's like leaving the seat belt unbuckled and trying to hold yourself in a roller-coaster car. The dips are too steep. You'll fall out! But you can trust God to keep you safe through the dips and twists of the wild ride of life. When life rushes by, hold onto God's truth. He will keep you safely moving forward on the track.

If something is troubling you, remember that God is right there with you. He is holding you securely. Even on the dips, you can trust Him. Let go, raise your hands, and enjoy the ride!

Let us Lift our HEART our & HANDS to GOD

~LAMENTATIONS 3:41~
NLT

GOD KEEPS ME BALANCED

I cried out, "I am slipping!" but your unfailing love, O LORD, supported me. When doubts filled my mind, your comfort gave me renewed hope and cheer.

PSALM 94:18–19 NLT

Gymnasts do amazing tricks on balance beams. They spin, flip, and tumble! Through each move, they must balance on a raised beam that is only four inches wide. It takes a lot of practice!

Are you facing a challenge that feels like a balancing trick? Maybe a sibling asked you to keep a secret from your parents. Perhaps two friends got in a fight and each one wants you to pick her side. Or maybe you made it onto the basketball team, but your best friend who tried out with you didn't. It's hard to know what to do in tricky situations. Your doubts can make you feel shaky inside. That's when you call out for a coach!

When gymnasts first learn to walk across the beam, they hold a coach's hand for support. Over time, gymnasts get better at balancing on their own. But when they learn a new trick, a coach will often support them with a hand. God is like a coach, always ready to hold your hand. He helps you along life's challenges and cheers you on as you get stronger. He supports you as you learn to stay balanced through tough choices. You can ask God for help at any moment, and He will reach out His hand. And if you fall, God is right there to comfort you and help you back up.

Hold onto God's hand and walk with confidence. Trust His support for each step. He will keep you balanced and steady through shaky events.

GOD SURPRISES ME

Whatever is good and perfect is a gift coming down to us from God our Father.

JAMES 1:17 NLT

*K*aboom! You watch a big firework explode in the sky. It glistens and rains down shimmering gold streaks. *Pop-POP!* Another firework bursts right next to it. It shoots out green and blue sparks in every direction. The whole sky dazzles with bright lights. It is the best show!

God likes to send you surprises that sparkle like fireworks. Everything seems quiet, then *pop!* Out of nowhere comes something exciting. Maybe you get a card in the mail. Or you hear that your grandparents are coming to visit. Or you see a shooting star. He loves to send you surprise blessings. They can be big or small. But each gift comes from Him.

God has a whole lineup of sparkling surprises for you. He loves to send reminders of His love and grace. His firework show is full of color. Each blessing He sends dazzles with His light and truth. God will burst through a normal day and excite you with something new and special. You can look forward to what He has in store for you. Next time you're surprised by something good, remember to thank God for His glistening gifts. Every good and perfect gift comes from Him.

Look around you. What blessings do you see? His show has already begun. Enjoy the colorful display of God's goodness. He gives the best surprises.

How is God blessing you right now? Make a list of His good surprises.

GOD TEACHES ME

Only the Lord gives wisdom. Knowledge and understanding come from him.

PROVERBS 2:6

Is there something that you've always wanted to learn? Maybe you'd like to play an instrument. Or you wish you knew how to ride a horse. It's easiest to learn something new from someone who is already an expert. And a good teacher will not only teach you well but get to know you too.

In the same way, God helps you learn. He is the greatest teacher because He is an expert at every topic. And He knows you very well. What do you want to learn? Maybe you want to be a better friend. Perhaps you need to practice patience. Or you want to better understand the Bible. Ask God, and He will teach you. He might teach you through the Bible, His Word. Other times, He will use people who also follow Him to teach you.

God is the very best teacher anyone could have. The more questions you ask, the more answers He provides. And when you make mistakes, He is patient and gentle to show you how to learn from them.

God has so many exciting topics to share with you. And you will learn only the right answers from Him. So go ahead and ask all your questions. As you listen to His answers, you will get to know Him better and learn to be wise like Him.

GOD COMFORTS ME

And he is the God of all comfort. He comforts us every time we have trouble, so that we can comfort others when they have trouble.

2 CORINTHIANS 1:3–4

Do you have a favorite stuffed animal? How does it make you feel when you hold it close? Maybe you feel warm inside. Or maybe you hold your stuffed animal when it's time for bed. It helps you relax and fall asleep. Do you ever share this stuffed animal with someone else so they can feel comforted too?

Like a special stuffed animal, God brings you comfort. Did you get picked on at school? Did a sibling say a hurtful word to you? Or is your coach putting pressure on you to play perfectly? Talk to God about it. He will hold you close and make you feel better.

Even though you can't hold God like you would a stuffed animal, your mind can hold onto His Word. You can also give God a hug by singing a worship song to Him. Or cuddle up to Him by sitting quietly and hearing what He has to say.

God's comfort also helps you comfort someone else. A friend might go through a similar situation later, and you will understand how they feel. You can share your story with them and tell them that God cares.

Do you need God's comfort today? Imagine wrapping your arms around Him and feeling warm inside. Hold Him close like you would a stuffed animal. Then tell others about how God wants to comfort them too.

GOD GROWS FAITH

So the one who plants is not important, and the one who waters is not important. Only God is important, because he is the One who make things grow.

1 CORINTHIANS 3:7

What are the steps for taking care of a garden? You need good soil. Seeds for planting. A fence to protect the plants from hungry animals sneaking in. Good sunlight. And a hardworking gardener to take care of the plants!

Like a gardener growing veggies, God grows faith. And He wants to use you as His gardening tool! Did you tell a friend about God? Do you wish your teacher knew about Jesus? Or maybe your church leader is encouraging you to share Jesus in your neighborhood. When you experience God's love, you want others to have it too. You can plant a seed of faith in others' hearts by telling them about God's love and grace. And you can water the seed by showing them what God's love looks like as you act with kindness. But you can't grow the seed. Only God can make faith sprout.

So don't be discouraged when you don't see growth after you've tried your best to plant seeds of faith in someone. It can take a long time to see a sprout. But even if you can't see it, God will tend that person's heart like a gardener fertilizing soil. He might use you to show your friend what it looks like to follow God. He might ask you to be kind to your teacher to show her an example of His compassion. Or He might show your neighbor His joy inside you when you play together. Only God can change people's hearts.

Remember that God is your gardener. He makes all things grow. He can also make others grow when you give them over to Him in prayer. He will always be tending His garden. Keep planting faith seeds. Keep watering others' hearts with love. One day, you'll see a bud!

As you color, think of someone you wish knew about God. Write their name on a vegetable. Give them to God in prayer. Ask Him to make their faith grow.

PROMISE 49

GOD GIVES ME HIS ARMOR

Wear the full armor of God. Wear God's armor so that
you can fight against the devil's evil tricks.

EPHESIANS 6:11

A rhinoceros's skin can be up to two inches thick! The tough skin covers rhinos' bodies like armor. Then they make their skin even stronger by rolling in mud. The mud adds a layer of protection from insect bites and sunburn. A rhino's armor is completed by its horn. Rhinos use this weapon against predators. Nothing can scare away a big rhino!

Like a rhino's armor of thick skin and threatening horn, God has given you spiritual armor. God's special armor has seven pieces to it. These parts prepare you to fight in the battle against sin:

- a belt of truth
- a chest plate of living right
- boots of peace
- a shield of faith
- a helmet of salvation
- a sword of God's Word
- prayer

You can wear your armor by telling the truth, doing what's right, living in peace, and believing in God. Sharpen your horn by reading the Bible and memorizing verses. Add a layer of protection like the rhino's coat of mud by praying every day. By doing these things, you can be confident that no evil can get through your armor. No doubt, lie, or sin can bite through your thick protection! Anytime an attacker comes charging at you, wear your armor and be safe in God.

GOD LOVES MY SONGS

Sing to the Lord a new song. Sing to the Lord, all the earth. Sing to the Lord and praise his name. Every day tell how he saves us.

PSALM 96:1–2

Whales make loud calls to communicate. The calls go up and down in pitch. And they have rhythm. The calls sound like the whales are singing! And these animals know how to lift their voices. Whale songs can be heard underwater over five hundred miles away!

God gave whales voices that make beautiful sounds. He loves to hear His creation sing—and that includes you! When you sing praise and worship songs, God loves to listen. Even if you sound like a whale!

Join the whales and sing a song to communicate with your Maker. Sing a song you've already memorized. Listen to a new worship song. Or make up your own song. God also likes it when you share songs with others, just like whales calling each other in the ocean. Share your song with your parent or best friend. And sing songs with others who love God. You'll be a pod of whales that make beautiful music!

There is no right way to sing to God. Sing loud and make your voice heard miles away. Or sing quietly by yourself. God just wants to hear your song.

There are many ways to express your love for God. Singing is a special way to communicate with Him. So join the chorus and sing a new song to your Creator. He loves to listen to your voice.

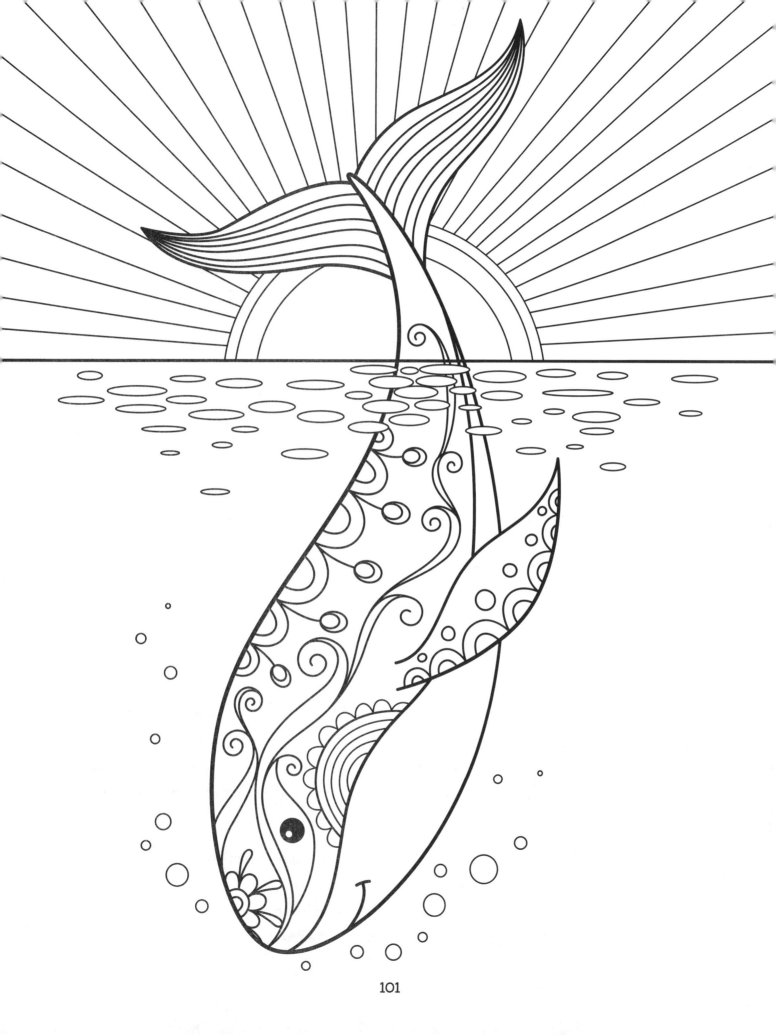

GOD WRITES MY STORY

You saw my body as it was formed. All the days planned for me were written in your book before I was one day old.

PSALM 139:16

A good story has an exciting beginning, a suspenseful middle, and a surprising end. It may have spaceships, unicorns, mermaids, or dragons. It might happen in a faraway world. And if it's a really good story, you'll want to read it right to the very end.

God's story for you is an epic adventure. Were you surprised when you heard that you got an award in school? Maybe you found out that your parents are having a baby or that your grandma lost her job. Events in life can be exciting and new, like riding a spaceship. They can also be challenging or scary, like fighting a dragon! God is with you through each surprise and tough situation. He counts your days like pages in a book. And each page is important to Him.

Through each new chapter, you can be a hero in God's story. When a friend congratulates you on the award, praise God for your talent. Then point out what your friend is good at. Care for your parents and new sibling with Christ's love by helping with extra chores. Encourage your grandma by being thankful when she buys you clothes at the resale shop to save money. Your story will have happy and sad parts. But in the end, it will be a wonderful tale of God's work. And remember, God can rewrite difficult beginnings into hopeful endings. He loves to make your story one big, exciting adventure.

The best part of your story when you follow Jesus is that your ending is just the beginning. When your story on earth is complete, you will spend forever with God in heaven. An ending with God is the happiest ending of all!

GOD CALLS ME BY NAME

Now this is what the Lord says . . . "Don't be afraid, because I have saved you. I have called you by name, and you are mine."

ISAIAH 43:1

It's the first day of school. The teacher asks you to write a name tag and decorate it. You grab a blue marker and draw waves under your name. Then you add a dolphin in the corner. Your teacher doesn't know that you love the ocean yet. But you're excited to share your name tag with the class.

A new teacher has to learn your name and all about you. She has to learn your favorite color. She'll find out what you want to be when you grow up. She will know you better and better each day. But there are also a lot of things she'll probably never know about you. On the other hand, God already knows all about you. Is your favorite food spaghetti? Do you like to take walks with your dog? Do you play the cello? What's important to you is also important to God. He loves everything about you.

Unlike being new to your teacher each school year, your name is always on God's roster. Your name is special to Him because you belong to Him as His child. When you talk to God, He always knows exactly who you are. He will never forget your name! And no matter what your name is, He pronounces it perfectly.

God pays a lot of attention to you. The next time your teacher calls your name in class, remember that God calls you too. He loves saying your name and speaks it with love.

Add your name to the name tag. Decorate it with pictures of your favorite things.

HELLO!

MY NAME IS...

I CAN DO BIG THINGS WITH GOD'S POWER

With God's power working in us, God can do much, much more than anything we can ask or think of.

EPHESIANS 3:20

What superpower do you wish you had? Maybe you want to fly above the clouds. Or to go back in time to the dinosaur days. A superpower would give you exciting new abilities. You could fight evil, complete secret missions, and save kittens! You could do many things you thought you could never do.

But if you follow Jesus, you already have the most super of powers inside you: God's Spirit. You can do so many amazing things with Him! Memorize a whole chapter from the Bible. Stand up for a bullied kid at school. Tell an adult about Jesus. Tell someone you're sorry. These are all big jobs! And you can complete them with God's power.

When you pray to God, He gives you super strength to do what's right. It's as if He hands you His cape! He can give you focus to memorize long scripture verses. He can give you courage to speak up to your teacher about a bully. He can give you just the right words to tell an adult what Jesus means to you. And He can remind you that He has already forgiven you when you have to say sorry. You might not feel like a superhero in these moments, but God's power is working inside you! He makes you able to do big things that would seem impossible without Him.

Ask God to help you use His superpowers. Ask Him to zap you with focus, courage, bravery, strength, and wisdom. What big job can you do with these new powers inside you? God can do much more than anything you can imagine.

I CAN TAKE MY TIME WITH GOD

God says, "Be still and know that I am God."

PSALM 46:10

Sloths are sooooo slooooow. It can take a whole minute for a sloth to crawl along a tree branch. These unique animals move slowly because they digest their food at the speed of, well, a sloth! It can take up to two weeks for a sloth's body to use all the energy in one meal. That means they don't have much spunk at one time. Try acting like a sloth for one minute. It's hard to be that slow!

You don't have to move at the speed of a sloth, but God wants you to slow down as you get to know Him. Do you have soccer practice each day of the week? Did your teacher assign a big school project? Are you swamped with homework from the week you missed class? Life can be busy! But it's important to press pause to spend time with God. Take a break between school and homework. Sit on a tree branch and tell God about your day. Read your Bible on the way to soccer practice. Or draw a picture about what God is teaching you before you start your project.

When life feels like it's running away, remember to slow down and hang out with God. Knowing Him is way more important than winning games or getting good grades. These slothy moments will give you energy to shine for God when you get to the next thing on your schedule. And if you're having trouble finding space for God time, talk to an adult about how to be less busy. Like one meal can keep a sloth moving for two weeks, God time is key to energizing your life.

GOD GIVES ME TALENTS

God has given each of you a gift from his great variety of spiritual gifts. Use them well to serve one another.

1 PETER 4:10 NLT

Do you have a favorite band or singer you listen to? Each instrument in a band has its own sound. A singer may have different instruments playing their song. Each instrument performs its own special part. A piano might be the first to begin. Then a bass guitar plucks a beat. Last, the drums pound! By itself, each instrument sounds okay. But when all the instruments play together, they make a beautiful song.

God has given you a special part to play in His band. What are you good at? Maybe you remember to pray for others each day. Or you always know how to make your friends feel loved. Or perhaps you're talented at cooking. God has given you these gifts. He wants you to use them to tell more people about Him.

Like the different notes in a piece of music, each person has their own part to perform. Together, we can play a song of God's goodness to the world. If you're skilled at cooking, show God's love to someone by baking them a treat. But your friend might be better at explaining how God's forgiveness works. Together you can sing a song of God's truth to a person who needs to hear about Him.

Talk to God about your talent. Ask Him to show you how to use it best. Then pick up your instrument and play your part. Only you can do the job He gives you. And He loves to hear the music that comes from using your gifts to tell others about Him.

I CAN BLESS OTHERS

Each one should give, then, what he has decided in his heart to give. . . . God loves the person who gives happily.

2 CORINTHIANS 9:7

Have you ever made a gift for a friend? When you gave your gift, your friend's face probably lit up with joy. They were so happy that you had thought of them. And giving them a gift made you happy too.

God loves to see you blessing others. Blessings are like gifts, but they aren't always wrapped in a bow. Have you ever helped an older person get something from a low shelf at the grocery store? Did your teacher ask you to help another classmate catch up on classwork they missed? Or maybe your teacher was out sick, so you made her a card. You have the power to bring joy to others! And that brings joy to God. He smiles when you make others smile. He loves to see you blessing others with a happy heart.

Sometimes you will help another person, and it won't go like you thought. Maybe you baked cookies for a neighbor, but he said that he was allergic and couldn't eat what you baked. Or you drew a picture for your little sibling, but she ripped it up the moment she put her hands on it. Not getting the reaction you expected can be frustrating. It can make you want to stop giving. But God sees your heart. And He loves a cheerful giver no matter what.

Remember, you can bless others. Give a present or just say a kind word. How will you bring someone a smile today? God will smile too.

How can you bless someone today? Make a list of ideas. Then try doing one!

GOD GIVES ME GOOD THOUGHTS

Don't copy the behavior and customs of this world, but let God transform you into a new person by changing the way you think.

ROMANS 12:2 NLT

Have you ever tried to untangle a ball of yarn? It twists into knots and more knots. You might start with the end of the string. You pull it, and the knot slowly starts to loosen. You keep pulling and unwinding each bunched-up knot one by one. Slowly, the whole ball of yarn starts to unravel. Finally, you can start to make that scarf!

Sometimes your thoughts can feel all tangled up like a knotted ball of yarn. Are you worrying about what you'll wear for the first day of school? Are you confused about why your parents keep fighting? Or are you frustrated by a friend who acts differently around other people? When hard things happen, your thoughts run here, there, and everywhere. They get knotted up with anger, negativity, and worry. But God wants to untangle your thoughts. He wants to make your thoughts straight and calm like His thoughts.

First God will find a thought that isn't from Him. He will unravel the tangled thought and pull it straight until it is true. He will also loosen knots of negative emotions with His loving presence. Then you will be able to think about what is true and right. Today, ask God to help you think more like Him. Then read some of His promises:

- I can have peaceful thoughts (Isaiah 26:3).
- I can think about things that are lovely and true (Philippians 4:8).
- I can make my thoughts obey Christ (2 Corinthians 10:4-6).

God can untangle your mind and unwind all the knots. He can even use your tangled ball of thoughts to craft your mind into something beautiful, like a scarf that keeps you warm and calm.

GOD WORKS FOR MY GOOD

We know that in everything God works for the good of those who love him.

ROMANS 8:28

Have you ever tasted the cocoa powder when you bake brownies? Yuck! By itself the powder is bitter. But once you mix it with flour, eggs, milk, sugar, and butter, it turns into sweet, chocolatey goodness.

Like a baker who uses sweet and bitter ingredients to make brownies, God uses the good and bad in your life to make you more like Him. Did you forget to read the chapters your teacher assigned? Is your ice hockey team losing all its games? Or are you having trouble making friends at school? Hard things in life can taste like bitter ingredients. Yuck! But God can mix together good from all the hard stuff. He will always add sweet ingredients to your life.

A missed assignment might make you really upset. But if you tell your teacher about the busy week you had, he might be gracious and give you another week to catch up. Losing games can feel awful. But you can enjoy the time with your teammates and learn a cool sport. And you might find a new friend who shares an interest when you join an after-school club.

God also uses the bitter things to make your faith stronger. Each difficultly is an opportunity to trust Him. Each rough day is a chance to taste His grace and love. God doesn't give you the bitter ingredients. But He will make sure there is a sweet treat from Him also. He is always working to add good things to your life. And His presence and friendship are the sweetest things of all!

TROUBLES produce PATIENCE and patience produces CHARACTER and character produces HOPE

~ROMANS 5:3-4~

I CAN DEPEND ON GOD

He never changes or casts a shifting shadow.

JAMES 1:17 NLT

Groundhog Day is a pretty silly holiday. Every year on February 2, people gather in Punxsutawney, Pennsylvania, to watch a groundhog come out of hibernation. There's a folktale that if the groundhog sees its shadow, it will mean six more weeks of winter. If it's cloudy and there is no shadow, spring is supposed to come early. It's fun to guess whether the groundhog's shadow will appear or not.

Shadows come and go, shrink and grow, shift and stretch. But God never changes. He never shifts or disappears like a shadow does. You can depend on Him each year to be the same God. And His presence isn't based on a folktale or weather pattern.

Did your parents ask you to change bedrooms? Are you donating all your old clothes and toys? Or maybe a parent is out of town for a business trip for a long time. Even though situations change in life, God never does. He is the same today as He was yesterday. And He'll be the same tomorrow and all the years ahead. You can count on God to be there for you. Rely on His words in Scripture. Depend on His Holy Spirit to guide you. You don't have to guess whether God will show up or not. He is with you when the sun goes down and when it shines brightly.

God will always be there for you. He isn't a folktale. You can depend on His presence. Unlike guessing whether the groundhog will see its shadow each year, you can count on seeing God every day, month, and year.

119

GOD USES ALL OF ME

Now may the God of peace make you holy in every way, and may your whole spirit
and soul and body be kept blameless until our Lord Jesus Christ comes again.

1 THESSALONIANS 5:23 NLT

Do you like to eat berries? Maybe your favorite berries are blackberries, raspberries, or even blueberries. Each one is juicy and delicious. You can use berries to make pies, sauces, and smoothies. And they're so easy to eat and cook because they don't need to be peeled or seeded. All the parts of a berry are good for eating. You just plop one into your mouth. Then you savor its sweet and ripe taste. Yum!

Like you can eat all parts of a berry, you can serve God with every part of yourself. You can use your voice to be a good leader and show others an example of living like Christ. You might use your courageous heart to tell a teacher about a bully. You can use your mind to remember the tasks your neighbors asked you to do to take care of their pet. God wants to use your mind, body, and heart to do His good work.

As you give your whole self to God, He will cleanse each part of you. Like washing off berries before eating them, God rinses away your sin. He will rinse off any selfishness or greed that gets in the way of being all in for Him.

Like a perfect berry with juicy fruit, thin skin, and tiny seeds, each part of you is valued by God. He will make you holy in every way when you give your whole self to Him. And He will savor your sweetness.

GOD MAKES ME SHINE

The wise people will shine like the brightness of the sky. Those who teach others to live right will shine like stars forever and ever.

DANIEL 12:3

The night sky is brimming with billions of stars. All you can see are white, sparkling lights. Then, out of nowhere, a shooting star flies across the sky. It catches your eye in just one moment. Your heart beats fast. You've been waiting to see this special sight, and you finally have!

Like a shooting star, you can shine too. You can be a light that shows the brightness of God's kindness, honesty, and care. Whose attention can you catch with your light? Do you have a younger brother or sister? Do you spend your weekends with your friends? God gives everyone a place to be a role model. He places you in a family or in a group of friends so you can set a good example for them. God might use you to tell your friends more about Him. Show them what it's like to put your trust in God or how to read Scripture or pray.

Today, ask God how you can shine for Him. Think of some places where you can be a role model. Then pray that God will help you be a good example for Him in these places. Brighten the sky with kindness and love. Like a shooting star, your example can draw others to God and what He's doing inside you. Your light will be too bright to look away!

As you color, think of places where you can be a role model. Write these places on the stars. Ask God to help you shine brightly.

I CAN RELAX WITH GOD

"Come to me, all of you who are tired and have heavy loads. I will give you rest."
MATTHEW 11:28

When you're in a hammock, you feel light. You're high up in the treetops. The hammock cradles your body, and you relax. The thick ropes knotted around the tree trunks will hold you securely.

Like a hammock supports your weight, God carries the things that make your heart heavy. He holds the weight of it all so that you can feel light and relaxed. This feeling comes from giving everything to Him in prayer. Your fears. Your mess-ups. The things that make you frustrated or annoyed. God will also hold up the people who you care about and pray for. He can lift it all. He wants you to rest knowing that He is the One holding all your heavy loads.

Part of relaxing in a hammock is trusting the ropes. Before you climb in, you have to attach the ropes safely to the trees. When you're sure the ropes are secure, you can fully relax your body. In the same way, trust God's words in the Bible. They are safe and will never loosen. Tie His words around your heart. Then climb in and relax in Him.

It's time to put up your hammock! Ask God to take your heavy load so you can fully rest in Him. Relax your body and let Him hold all the weight.

GOD MAKES ME NEW

But you were taught to be made new in your hearts. You were taught to become a new person. That new person is made to be like God—made to be truly good and holy.

EPHESIANS 4:23–24

Don't you feel snazzy in a shiny new pair of shoes? Your old pair didn't fit anymore. They were dingy, worn, and starting to tear. It was time for an upgrade. And a different color. Now in your new pair, you have a fresh pep to your step!

God wants to add a pep to your step that feels way better than new shoes. When you choose to follow Him, He will make you a shiny new person. He will help you replace the old behaviors that don't fit you anymore with new ones that show His colorful love. Is it hard to be kind to your classmates? Do you have trouble obeying your parents? Or are you and a sibling fighting a lot? When you keep doing things your old way, you get worn out like a pair of old shoes.

But God can remove the wear and tear from your heart and make it whole again. He will show you ways to act more like Him. He will help you make good choices and be kind to others. He might show you how to love your classmates better. He might give you kind words to say to your parents. Or He might teach you how to care for your sibling. God will help you trade in your old behaviors for new, polished ones.

Let God replace your worn and torn old ways. Ask Him to make you a new person. Put on what He hands you back. Then walk forward with confidence. You're bright and new!

If you could have a new pair of shoes, what would
they look like? Draw your shoes below.

I AM ON GOD'S MIND

How precious are your thoughts about me, O God. They cannot be numbered! I can't even count them; they outnumber the grains of sand!

PSALM 139:17–18 NLT

Imagine a sandcastle one foot tall and one foot wide. Can you guess how many grains of sand are in the castle? Counting every grain of sand one by one would be impossible. But it turns out there would be about a *billion* grains of sand in a sandcastle that size. Now, imagine a whole beach of sand. That would be billions and billions and billions of sand grains.

God thinks about you more times than the number of all the grains of sand on all the beaches in the world. Not even the smartest mathematician could count that high! And God's thoughts about you are good. He thinks you're amazing and fun to be around. He loves the way you smile and laugh. And He can't wait to see you chase your dreams! You are on God's mind even when you don't think about Him. It makes Him happy to think about you.

It feels good when you find out you were on someone's mind. Don't you just love getting a card in the mail or finding a note in your lunchbox? You can always read a note from God. Here are some of the things He thinks about you:

- God wants me to live with Him forever (John 14:2-3).
- God calls me great in the kingdom of heaven (Matthew 5:19).
- God says I'm His peacemaker (Mathew 5:9).
- I am a friend of Jesus (John 15:13-14).

Imagine building the biggest sandcastle *ever*. Each of the grains you use to make your castle is a thought from God. You could never get close to counting them all. He thinks about you this much and more.

GOD GIVES ME GOOD NEWS

Now, brothers, I want you to remember the Good News I brought to you. You received this Good News, and you continue strong in it. And you are saved by this Good News.

1 CORINTHIANS 15:1–2

There's a song faintly playing outside your bedroom window. The notes get louder and louder. The tune is familiar—it's the ice cream truck! The song announces the joyous arrival of frozen treats. Now that's good news!

God has brought you good news too. His announcement is the Good News of Jesus. It means the forgiveness of all your sins. Because Jesus died on the cross for you, you don't have to be perfect to get to heaven. If you follow Jesus, God forgives all your mistakes. It's the very best news you could ever hear!

Did you know that God announced His Good News with a song too? When Jesus was born, angels sang about the baby to shepherds. The shepherds then went right to the stable to see Jesus! But the Good News of Jesus is much bigger than the notes to a song. His saving forgiveness plays in your heart. It rings loud and never stops.

God still uses music to share the Good News of Jesus. You can help spread the news by singing praise songs. Or by telling someone about the forgiveness Jesus offers. Whenever you hear the notes of God's Good News, run to Jesus and enjoy the refreshing treat of His salvation. He is the best news you will ever hear and the most important news you will ever share.

GOD SAYS I'M WORTHY

"When birds are sold, two small birds cost only a penny. But not even one of the little birds can die without your Father's knowing it. . . . So don't be afraid. You are worth much more than many birds."

MATTHEW 10:29–31

What is your favorite type of bird? A falcon? A blue jay? Maybe a pink flamingo. Or perhaps a colorful talking parrot! Some people have pet parrots that come from other parts of the world. Their feathers can be bright blue, golden yellow, or even cherry red. These beautiful pets require lots of good care. And they can be very expensive. Some parrots cost thousands of dollars. Better not let one of those fly out a window!

God knows each bird that flaps through the sky or hops in a cage. He sees them fly. He hears them sing. He knows the color of every feather. But God says you're worth more than any bird—even a rare parrot that costs more than all the chore money you will ever earn.

God values you so much! And no matter where you fly, your value will never be lost. God sees you play and run. He hears you laugh. He knows each strand of hair and every finger. God values every part of you. Like a pet owner loves a parrot, God will take good care of you.

You are worth a lot to God—more than all the birds in the world combined. Nothing will ever be more precious to Him. Every part of you is special. And He takes good care of what's valuable to Him.

GOD IS WITHIN REACH

In Christ we can come before God with freedom and without fear. We can do this through faith in Christ.

EPHESIANS 3:12

Giraffes reach their dinner in the treetops with their six-foot-long necks. They also use their twenty-one-inch-long tongues to grab leaves. Giraffes' long tongues reach around sharp thorns and pointy branches. The tastiest leaves are within reach.

In the same way a giraffe's body makes it able to reach its food, Jesus brings you within reach of God. And you can grab onto Him whenever you want. He is never too high up or too far away. Are you going to church for the first time? Did you get a new Bible? Maybe you've heard about God before, but you don't know if He really hears your prayers.

When you place your faith in Jesus, He forgives the sins that separate you from God. You can go to God freely and receive whatever He wants to give you. When you reach for God, you can grab onto His peace. You can grab onto His love. You can grab onto His words in the Bible. You can reach for Him without fear of any sharp thorns or pointy branches. God is right there. And He hears every prayer you make.

Stretch toward God as you read a new scripture. Reach up to Him by listening to a worship song. Grab onto Him through prayer. Like a giraffe munching in the treetops, you can always reach for God. He is near.

GOD'S WAYS ARE HIGHER

Just as the heavens are higher than the earth, so are my ways higher than your ways. And my thoughts are higher than your thoughts.

ISAIAH 55:9

You look up. A tall building seems to disappear into the clouds. There are many floors that lead to the top. It is so high that the reflection of the whole city gleams in the windows.

God's ways are higher than the tallest building or skyscraper. His thoughts reach beyond the clouds. Just as the designer knows the location of every door and stairway on each floor, God sees much more than you do. And like the builder knows how much concrete and steel to use at the building's base to support the whole weight, God understands exactly what you need. Maybe you wonder why an answer to your prayers isn't coming. Or you're confused why one person got better from an illness but another didn't. It's frustrating when you don't understand what's going on around you.

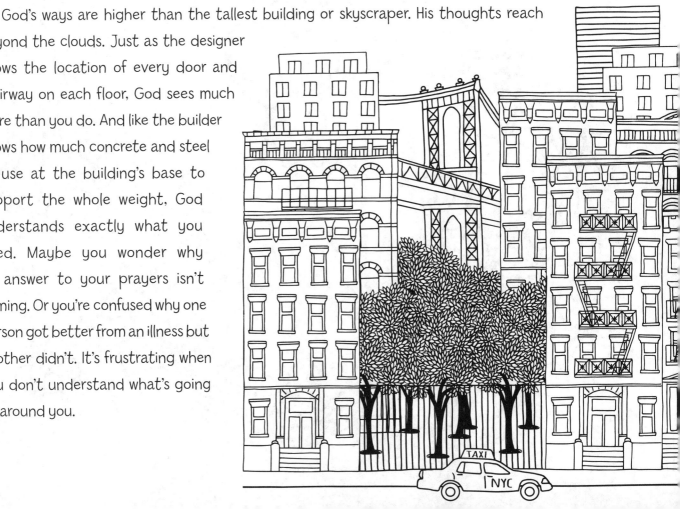

But you don't have to understand everything. God sees every part of the problem. He understands exactly what's needed to bear the weight of His plans. And He understands you better than you know yourself. God's ways are too big for us to see. But they are always good. They are higher—better—than any thoughts you could ever think. That's because they always reflect His love.

Like a person standing on the ground floor of a building, you can see only part of the picture. But God sees every floor from the inside and outside all at once. He knows exactly how to build up to the sky. So don't be frustrated. Remember that when you are confused, God knows what's going on. His ways are higher.

GOD ANSWERS MY CALL

I call to you in times of trouble. You certainly will answer me.

PSALM 86:7

Do you use video chat to communicate with friends and family? Maybe you like to call your best friend to hear how they're doing. Or you call your grandparents each week to tell them everything you did. Using the internet to share your adventures keeps you in touch with the people you love!

God wants to hear from you too. Like your best friend or grandparent, He is curious about your day and all your adventures. Even though God already knows these things, He likes to hear you talk about them. And He is always available. He will answer your call every time. Is today a hard day? Are you feeling excited about an upcoming play that you have a part in? Or maybe you just want someone to talk to. God will pick up your call. You can share anything with Him.

Call God by praying to Him. Or write your thoughts in a journal. You can even call God by just sitting quietly and thinking about Him. He will answer you no matter how you call Him. He loves to see your face and hear your voice. When you call on God, He will respond. He might give you a Bible verse to read that will encourage your heart. He might laugh with you about exciting things. Or He might just listen.

What are you waiting for? Give God a call. He will answer right away.

In the speech bubbles, write or draw all the things you want to tell God today.

I CAN FIND JOY IN GOD

You will teach me God's way to live. Being with you will fill me
with joy. At your right hand I will find pleasure forever.

PSALM 16:11

What do you do when it's sunny outside? Do you have a water balloon fight or play a ball game? Maybe you chalk your sidewalk with doodles. Or you go on a long hike. Being in the sun can feel so good, especially after it's been rainy for many days. When it's finally sunny again, you run outside and feel the warmth of the rays!

Like having fun in the sun, you can have fun with God. You can talk to Him wherever you go and tell Him all the wonderful things you see. You can share stories of how God has answered your prayers with your family and friends. It's exciting to follow God! In fact, He wants you to enjoy life (Ecclesiastes 8:15). And His words about you in the Bible can also bring happiness to your heart. Here are some ways God can brighten your day with His joy:

- Read your favorite scripture verse.
- Draw a picture of what you're thankful for.
- Talk to God out loud while going on a walk.
- Sing or dance to a worship song.

Joy is like happiness, but they're not the same thing. You can feel joy even when you're feeling sad or discouraged. Maybe a family vacation you were looking forward to got canceled. Or your sports season is now over and you'll miss all your teammates. Pray to

God about these things. Ask Him for His joy. He will remind you of how much you mean to Him. And that's reason to celebrate! No matter how gloomy the day, God loves to bring you smiles.

Find a way to celebrate with God, and have fun praising Him! Forget about any troubles that darken your day like rain clouds. Let His joy warm your heart like sun rays on your face.

GOD BRIGHTENS MY LIFE

"My purpose is to give them a rich and satisfying life."

JOHN 10:10 NLT

Adding color to a black-and-white picture brings it to life! If everything is gray, you can't tell what color someone's hair or shirt is. You can't tell if it's sunset or midday. Bright flowers get lost in the leaves. But a color picture brings all these details to life. It tells a rich and full story!

Like adding color to a black-and-white picture, God adds color to your life. He wants your days to be full of rich and beautiful things that satisfy your heart. Your life becomes rich when you decide to follow God. He brightens your heart with His complete love, grace, and so much more. It's like adding new colors to a black-and-white photo.

But God doesn't stop there. He sends you beautiful things each day. He makes your life bright! You might walk past yellow flowers in your neighborhood or see a rainbow on your way to school. Maybe you discover a new favorite author. Or perhaps you get a hug from your teacher. Watch for these small bits of beauty. They are all blessings from God to add colorful goodness to your life. God wants your life to be just as beautiful as the colors you see in the world.

Thank God for giving you a full life as His child. Praise Him for His rich love that satisfies your soul and colors your heart. And don't forget to notice all the bits of beauty He adds to each day. God loves brightening your life!

GOD SURROUNDS ME

The Lord surrounds his people now and forever.

PSALM 125:2

A fence tells those walking by, "This is mine." A fence might surround a garden to protect vegetables from being eaten by critters. It might surround a front yard to keep kids and pets off someone's grass. Or a fence might pen in sheep on a farm. A fence can be high and long or short and low. It can surround a huge apartment building or just one house. But each fence has the same job. It guards whatever is inside.

God surrounds you like a tall, strong fence. He says, "This child is mine!" God might give you calm thoughts before bed to help you fall asleep. He might remind you of a scripture verse about forgiving others when your feelings are hurt. Or He might bring you good news that you didn't expect to remind you that He is listening to your prayers. God encircles you with His presence. Wherever you look, you can see Him. His Word goes all the way around you. It is strong and high.

Sometimes, fences will get old and need repairing. They might fall over in a strong wind or need a fresh coat of paint to look good again. But God's protection will never weaken. He will continue to stand strong and tall around you. Keep trusting His Word. It never wobbles or falls. And His love will never need a refresh.

God surrounds you. He is a sturdy fence of protection.

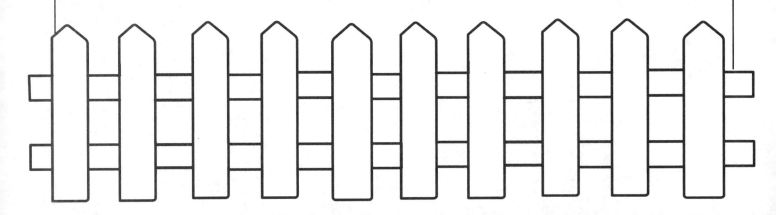

I CAN FORGIVE OTHERS

Hatred stirs up trouble. But love forgives all wrongs.

PROVERBS 10:12

The ocean waves roll in and out, in and out. Each new wave breaks onto the shore. Then it pulls back, leaving the sand underneath soft and smooth. The next wave repeats the pattern. Over and over again. The rhythm creates a peaceful sound.

Forgiveness is like the ocean sending waves against the shore. It should happen again and again. God's perfect grace forgives you repeatedly. And God teaches us to forgive others in the same way.

Forgiving someone who hurt you is hard. But remember that God has already forgiven you. He wants you to follow His example and forgive others. Just like He forgives you again each day, you can forgive others. Did a friend say a hurtful word to you? Ask God to help you forgive. He will soften your heart like the ocean smooths sand. Let the wave of His grace roll over you. Soak it up. Then you can give God's grace to others. When you forgive someone, God will wash away the hurt and make your heart smooth again.

God's forgiveness is like the waves. It will never stop. His mercy will wash over you repeatedly. That's why you should treat others the same way and forgive them. Over and over again. You can choose to forgive. Each time you do, a peaceful rhythm will roll over your heart.

GOD CARES ABOUT MY NEEDS

My God will use his wonderful riches in Christ Jesus to give you everything you need.

PHILIPPIANS 4:19

A water hole is a pool of water where animals drink. In Africa, elephants, giraffes, and zebras travel to water holes in the dry savanna grasslands. These animals will walk long distances to find a hole. They know it will supply them with the water they need to survive.

God placed water holes in the savanna to care for His creatures. And He cares about your needs too. Do you need forgiveness for treating someone badly? Is your pantry almost empty? Are you sad about moving to a new grade and saying goodbye to your old teacher? These are all needs. And God cares about each one.

God cares when people need food or a safe home. He also cares about how people feel. He hates it when someone is sad or worried. He is your Father in heaven, and He cares what happens to you. Ask for His help. Then wait and watch what He does. God might give you hope when you feel sad. Or He might use other people to give money or food to someone who needs it. And He will always supply you with His love, grace, and presence. You need those above all!

God wants to care for you. And you don't have to travel long distances to receive His help. He is already beside you. Give Him your needs, and receive His tender loving care.

GOD LOOKS OUT FOR ME

The Lord looked down from heaven at all the people. He looked to see if anyone was wise, if anyone was looking to God for help.

PSALM 14:2

Imagine that you climb up into a treehouse way high in the branches. What might you see from up there? You see your parent's car coming down the street to your house. And you notice your friend falling off their bike. Ouch! Being high up lets you see a lot. You feel on top of the world.

God looks down from above too. He watches you from heaven. And He loves to see everything you do. Are you looking after your baby brother? Do you water the flowers you planted? Or maybe you have a fish that you feed. We look after things that are important to us here on earth. And God looks after the earth and everything in it—including you!

Like seeing the people below in your neighborhood, God knows about the things happening around you. He knows that the answers to your prayers are on their way. He sees when your friend needs help. God knows all that happens on earth. And all the while, His eyes stay on you!

God loves to watch you go about your day. And when you need Him, He is already looking out for you.

GOD'S ANSWERS ARE WORTH THE WAIT

Wait for the Lord's help. Be strong and brave and wait for the Lord's help.

PSALM 27:14

What's the longest time you've had to wait for something? Did it feel impossible to wait? Maybe you were expecting a package in the mail. You ordered a new toy with your birthday money. Or a relative said they were sending you a box of homemade goodies. You checked your doorstep every few minutes. Nope. No package today. Waiting is harder than you thought!

Like waiting for a package to arrive, sometimes you have to wait for God to answer your prayers. You might not understand why you're having to wait or what's delaying God's response. But God knows what's best. He has perfect timing.

While you wait on God, you can trust Him. Whatever God delivers will be good. You may not know what is coming, but you know that God sends only good packages. Just like that relative who sends the best treats. Are you praying for a friend to know Jesus? Does your church leader need physical healing? Ask God for help. Then trust His timing as you wait. He might give you just the right opportunity to share about Him with your friend. Or He might teach you about patience as you let Him take care of your church leader.

Wait for the Lord. He will deliver the very best goodies when the time is right. His answer is on the way!

What answer to prayer are you waiting on? Write it on a package. Ask God for patience, and thank Him for the answer that is on its way.

I CAN FIND GOD

"You will search for me. And when you search for me with all your heart, you will find me!"
JEREMIAH 29:13

What's the coolest bug you've ever found? It's fun to search for tiny insects. Bugs hide under rocks and plant leaves. They take cover inside empty pots and between cracks in the cement. These small creatures are good at hiding. You might even have to use a magnifying glass to see the tiniest ones.

Like scouting for cool bugs, you can search for God. And He is much easier to find than tiny insects. Have you ever wondered what it's like to follow God? Maybe your friend asked you a tough question about the Bible. Or you aren't sure how to pray. You might wonder if you're supposed to feel differently or if something should change when you talk to Him.

God says that if you seek Him with all your heart, you will find Him. He wants to answer all your questions. Tell Him what's on your mind and heart, and He will help you see the things He's doing around you. You can also find God by reading the Bible. You will see Him in the stories that show His love and grace for His children. God isn't trying to hide from you like a scurrying bug.

Search for God. You will find Him! He is much easier to discover than tiny bugs. You don't even need a magnifying glass.

GOD KEEPS ME STEADY

Crying may last for a night. But joy comes in the morning.

PSALM 30:5

Clouds can change quickly. They form different shapes depending on the temperature and how much water they hold. The wind can blow clouds together or pull them apart. A small cloud may join a larger cloud. Or it might float away on its own.

Like these shifting puffs in the sky, your emotions can change quickly. One moment you feel happy. Then all of a sudden you feel sad. You might give your sibling a warm hug one minute. But soon you're chasing them with clenched fists. Like the wind blowing clouds around, events in your life can quickly shift your feelings. Your emotions can go from a light puff of cheerfulness to a thick fog of gloom.

No matter how your feelings change, remember that God remains the same. He still loves you. He still sends you good things—even when it feels like everything is going wrong. Stay steady in the shifting wind of your emotions by remembering God's Word. His truths don't blow away or change shape.

Like clouds passing by in the sky, your emotions will pass with time. Are you feeling gloomy today? Are you full of laughter and giggles? Give your emotions to God. Every feeling matters to Him, even if it's one you need to let float away.

Like clouds come and go, your feelings come and go too. Read God's Word to feel steady again. God understands every emotion you feel. You and He can watch the clouds pass by together.

What are you feeling today? Draw a cloud in the shape of that emotion as you tell God how you feel. If it's an emotion you need to let drift away, ask God to help you send it into the sky.

I CAN EXERCISE MY FAITH

I can do all things through Christ because he gives me strength.

PHILIPPIANS 4:13

What fun things can you do to exercise? How about one hundred jumping jacks? Or maybe you like to take your dog on walks. Make sure to stretch before any workout! Take a few gulps of water. Munch on a snack for energy. These steps get your muscles ready to go.

Like strong muscles, God wants your faith ready to go. He has big tasks for you! And just as your body needs to move and stretch, your faith needs exercise to be healthy and strong.

Faith exercise is a lot like lifting weights or doing jumping jacks. Doing a little each day makes you stronger and stronger. There are lots of ways to build up your faith. Read your Bible, pray, and worship. You can also go to church, be part of a Bible study, and share your faith with others.

Another way to exercise your faith is by practicing trust. Have you ever done a trust fall? One person falls backward until another person catches them. The person falling has to trust that their partner will catch them! You can do trust falls with God. Think of one thing that you need to practice trust about. Then give it to God each morning. If you start to worry about it, let it fall back into God's hands.

It's time to exercise. Stand up. Stretch those muscles. Pick up your Bible or a prayer journal. Turn on a worship song. Practice telling someone about what God has done for you. Let something that troubles you fall into God's hands. Each time you practice, your faith will grow a little stronger.

GOD CAN'T BE MEASURED

Our Lord is great and very powerful. There is no limit to what he knows.

PSALM 147:5

Do you use a height chart to keep track of how tall you get? Your parent might mark a line on the wall and write your age. Then next time you measure, you can see how much you've grown. It feels good when you reach the next inch or foot on the chart. You're getting so big!

No matter how tall you get, your height will always come out in feet and inches. But there are no measuring units that can show God's size. He has no beginning and no end. His knowledge is more than can be measured. And no one can mark what He does!

Because there is no limit to what God knows, you can trust what He says to be true. You can believe His Word because God has all the brains in the world and more. He won't ever make a mistake. Everything He does is based on His complete knowledge. No one else can even keep track of what He knows. He does miracles that no one else can describe or understand. And He knows all the answers to your questions. He wants to show you new things.

God doesn't grow in inches or feet. He is already too big to be measured. You'll never reach the limit of what He knows or can do. You can always go to Him to learn something new.

GOD IS MY GOOD FATHER

The Father has loved us so much! He loved us so much that we are called children of God. And we really are his children.

1 JOHN 3:1

Penguins are great dads. A male penguin holds an egg for weeks and weeks. He keeps the egg warm, nestled on top of his feet and under his feathery belly. He never lets go so that no predator can snatch the egg. He will also feed the new chick when it hatches. The father cares for the egg because it is his job. He loves his chick.

Like a male penguin cares for his chick, God is a good Father. If you follow Jesus, you are God's child. He loves to take care of you. And He's the greatest Dad in the world! God is a good Father because He holds you close to Him. He keeps your heart warm when you talk to Him or listen to a worship song. When you're nestled in Him, you are completely safe. Nothing can snatch you out of His grip. He also feeds you with His Word. When you read the Bible, He nourishes your spirit with His truth. Most of all, God loves you with a great big Daddy kind of love.

You are God's child. He is your Dad! He will hold you close. He is a perfect Father, and He takes the very best care of you.

GOD RESCUES ME

"He reached down from heaven and rescued me; he drew me out of deep waters. He rescued me from my powerful enemies."

2 SAMUEL 22:17–18 NLT

Imagine that you're a shipwrecked sailor. You're swimming out at sea, but your arms are getting tired. The waves are getting bigger. Then out of nowhere, a dolphin swoops underneath you! Your head lifts up above the water. You hold onto the dolphin's fin as it pulls you back to shore. Now that would be cool!

Like a dolphin rescuing someone from drowning, God will save you from sinking under problems that feel as deep as the ocean. He will be the first to respond when you're needing help. Is your family drowning in arguments? Maybe you're struggling to keep your head above all your schoolwork. Or you feel like you're swimming alone after your best friend moved away. Ask God to rescue you. Tell Him all about the problem in your life that feels like a shipwreck. He will come from underneath you and lift you out of the deep water.

When you call out to God, He will come close. Like holding onto a dolphin's fin in the middle of the ocean, you can cling to God. He will support you with His strength.

God hates to see you in trouble. The next time you feel like you're drowning in a problem, pray to God. He will come to you. You don't have to fear the waves of trouble in life. God will swoop underneath you and rescue you. His grace and love will take you back to shore.

I CAN SMELL LIKE JESUS

God uses us to spread his knowledge everywhere like a sweet-smelling perfume. Our offering to God is this: We are the sweet smell of Christ among those who are being saved and among those who are being lost.

2 CORINTHIANS 2:14–15

What's your favorite flower? Now imagine one hundred of those flowers. They are freshly cut and all bunched together. They smell sweet and fruity. You plunge your nose into the entire bunch. Take a big sniff. Don't sneeze! The sweet scent fills your nostrils. You're going to give the whole bouquet to someone special to show your love.

Like giving someone a sweet-smelling bouquet of lavender, roses, or peonies, you can give others the beautiful scent of God. Did you help a friend? Did you say "thank you" to your teacher? Did you tell a neighbor how you came to know God? God loves it when you spread the beautiful scent of His love and truth.

When people see you acting with God's love, they will want to come closer to you. You're showing them that God smells sweet, just like a bouquet. And they just might want to know more about Christ.

You can draw others closer to God by sharing His sweet and fruity scent. When people come close to investigate your sweetness, tell them it comes from God. And tell them that He can make them as fresh as flowers too!

How can you share God with others by being sweet? Journal your ideas.

_____

_____

_____

I CAN MAKE MEMORIES WITH GOD

Remember the wonderful things he has done. Remember his miracles and his decisions.

1 CHRONICLES 16:12

It's fun to look back on favorite moments by looking at photos or watching videos. Maybe you went on a camping trip and caught your first fish. Your grandma shot a video of your big, slimy prize. Or you visited family in a different state and flew on an airplane. Your dad took a picture of your excited face boarding the plane. By saving photos and videos, you make sure the best moments in your life are never forgotten!

Like remembering accomplishments or vacations, you can remember your special times with God. When has God done something for you that you will never forget? Maybe He gave you courage to score a home run in a softball game last week. Or He helped you say sorry to your parent only to hear them tell you how much they love you. You felt God's love in these moments. Keep them in your heart and thank God for them.

You can also remember what God has done in other people's lives. When you read Bible stories, you learn about people who experienced God in great ways. The Bible is full of memories that should never be forgotten!

Like making a photo album or posting videos on social media, you can save your best memories with God. Here are some ideas:

- Keep a praise journal.
- Draw pictures in a sketchbook.

- Highlight passages and write notes in your Bible.
- Make a faith scrapbook with photos and notes.
- Record videos of you talking about your special moments.

Share your memory collection with someone. And don't forget to ask them to share their memories too! Your faith grows when you celebrate what God has done with others.

Think about a time God did something special for you. Draw this memory inside the photo frame. Thank God for the wonderful memories He gives you!

GOD TAKES MY PLACE

Christ had no sin. But God made him become sin. God did this for us so that in Christ we could become right with God.

2 CORINTHIANS 5:21

Stunt doubles do the most dangerous job on a movie set. They are trained to fight, flip through the air, and drive cars in chases. A stunt double takes the place of a star actor when the character must do something dangerous. Stunt doubles do the tricky stuff so that actors don't get hurt.

Like a stunt double takes the place of a movie star, Jesus took your place on the cross. He kept you out of danger by taking the punishment for your sin. Because of Jesus' death, God will forgive your mistakes. All you have to do is ask Jesus to come into your heart and save you. Then you won't have to worry about where you'll end up when you die. He gives you a forever home in heaven. Talk about a safe place to shine!

Jesus also takes your place by fighting evil for you. You don't have to worry about Satan's tricks or the evil in your heart. Let God throw the punches. He is the expert on battling sin.

Ask Jesus to be your replacement today. Ask Him to forgive your sins. He has already paid the punishment on the cross! Then promise to follow Him for the rest of your life. When you let Jesus be your double, He comes into your heart to help you act out your role in life.

He LOVED ME and GAVE HIMSELF to SAVE me

~GALATIANS 2:20~

GOD NEVER WASTES WHAT I GIVE HIM

Always give yourselves fully to the work of the Lord. You know that your work in the Lord is never wasted.

1 CORINTHIANS 15:58

Imagine you've been asked to invent a robot out of recycled pieces. You visit a junkyard to collect materials. You find scraps of wood for the body. Old shopping cart wheels will move your robot around. Four old pipes will make arms and legs. And an old rope will top off your creation with silly hair. Your robot is coming to life!

Like recycling old scraps to build a robot, God can use the messy and forgotten things in your life. Do you have to retake a quiz? Do you have to write thank-you notes for gifts you don't even like? Or maybe you have chores to do at home. God can use the things that feel small or useless to you. No scrap is ever wasted when you try your best for Him. He uses every part of your life.

When you let God collect each minute of your day, He will build something amazing. He might give you a new friend on the late bus when you stay after school to retake the quiz. He might help you discover cool things about your aunt when she writes you a letter back. Or He might use you to encourage your parent when they come home to cleaned dishes. God loves to invent new things out of the scraps you give Him. Nothing is too boring to Him. He will show you a fun-filled life even when you give Him the parts that feel useless.

What jobs has God given you today? Do your best. Then watch what He can turn them into. God makes the most amazing inventions!

Complete the picture. Can you add pieces of junk that make the robot even better?

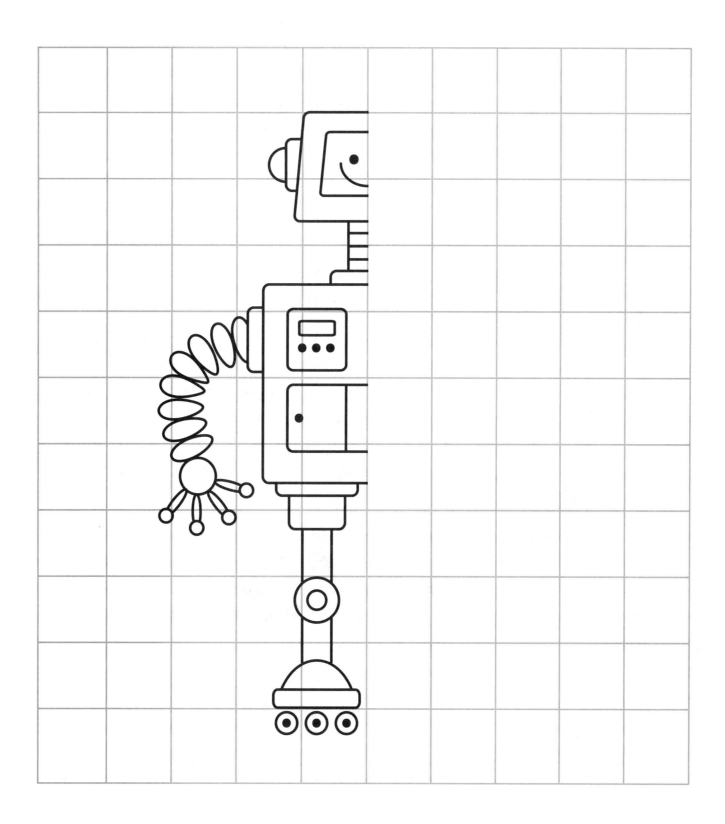

GOD SETS ME FREE

So Jesus said . . . "If you continue to obey my teaching, you are truly my followers. Then you will know the truth. And the truth will make you free."

JOHN 8:31–32

Sea turtles hatch from eggs in the sand. When they are born, they must crawl to the ocean. But that is a daring task. Predators like birds and crabs snatch baby turtles as they scurry toward the waves. Thank goodness for turtle patrollers! These volunteers watch turtle nests for hatchlings. Then they scare off predators so the little turtles can make it into the water. The happy hatchlings swim away free!

Like a baby sea turtle, you can swim through life in freedom. Sin is like a tight shell that keeps you from reaching the ocean-blue joys of life. But when you accept God's truth about Jesus, He breaks your shell of sin. You can swim freely into the wonderful new blessings God is hatching for you. You might discover a talent when you help with a service project. You can read the Bible and be amazed at His miracles. And you can say no to temptation because you know God's way is better.

And God will continue to set you free. Some sea turtles get caught in trash once they're in the ocean. They get stuck again. Sin is like the trash floating in the sea. Maybe you said you ate your broccoli but you snuck it to the dog. Or you told a friend that you didn't want to see them anymore. Or you promised to say only kind words, but then your sibling made you sooo mad. God will free you from the trap of sin again.

Jesus' forgiveness sets you free to live out the adventure God has for you. You'll be like a sea turtle swimming in the ocean, just as God designed it to do. Follow Jesus into fun and freedom.

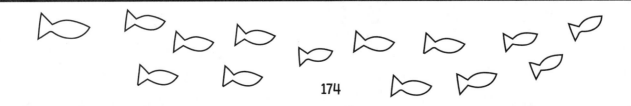

GOD MOVES IN ME

So we set our eyes not on what we see but on what we cannot see. What we see will last only a short time. But what we cannot see will last forever.

2 CORINTHIANS 4:18

In the fall, the wind turns cool. Gusts blow your hair. You pull on a sweater or jacket. You can't see the wind, but you can feel it. You also notice its work. It blows the falling leaves in colorful whirlwinds. It carries the smell of cinnamon out of a kitchen window.

Like looking for the wind, it's hard to see what God is up to. You might wonder if He is still close by. Is He still doing good things for you? But God is always moving. He might blow a cool breeze on your anger and help you calm down. He might whisk away a fear and help you have confidence in who He made you to be. Slowly but surely, He makes you more and more like Him—just like the wind will smooth a rock's surface over many years.

Even though you can't see God's work, it will last forever. You will bring the gentleness, boldness, and truth He carries into your heart with you into heaven. These things matter more to God than accomplishments, such as a perfect test score or a win for your swim team. These things will blow away like brown leaves. But a heart filled with His love will remain as solid as a tree trunk.

Watch for God's work. Is He blowing away your selfishness like dead leaves? Does your heart feel a light autumn breeze when you worship? He is always moving in you. Like the windy fall season, God brings change to your life and replaces your old sinful habits with bright, colorful new ways of thinking and acting.

GOD DOES THE UNTHINKABLE

God rescues and saves people. God does mighty miracles in heaven and on earth.

DANIEL 6:27

Have you ever wondered how magicians perform their tricks? They can do incredible things like pull a rabbit out of an empty top hat. They can make a red handkerchief disappear. They can even name a card that you secretly picked and didn't show anyone! Magicians fool their audiences into looking at one thing while they operate the trick somewhere else. That's why magic tricks are called *illusions*. They look like something they are not.

Like a magician uses tricks to make an illusion, God can perform the unthinkable. But His acts are completely real. They are called *miracles*. You can read about many miracles in the Bible: God parted a giant sea for Moses and the Israelites to cross and escape the army chasing them. He kept Daniel safe from a den of hungry lions. And Jesus healed people from illness. God's awesome deeds deserve the loudest round of applause.

Only God has the power to do miracles. And they aren't meant to lead your eyes somewhere else. Instead God's amazing feats lead you to the truth—Him! His biggest miracle is rescuing and saving people. He speaks to someone's heart until they choose to follow Him. He forgives anyone who asks and lets them live forever with Him in heaven.

Nothing God does is an illusion. It's all real! So ask Him for anything. He will hear you even when you pray in secret. He might do a miracle like in the Bible, or He might do a miracle in your heart. God will show Himself to you in a mighty way, even if His answer takes time or looks different than you expected. Remember, God can perform the unthinkable. In big ways and small ways, He does amazing deeds.

GOD GIVES ME PEACE OF MIND

"I leave you peace. My peace I give you. I do not give it to you as the world does. So don't let your hearts be troubled. Don't be afraid."

JOHN 14:27

It's humid out and the bugs are swarming. *Spritz!* You spray repellant all over your body. It keeps the mosquitoes from landing on you. *Whack! Whack!* Your fly swatter slaps away the bugs that buzz around your head. Sometimes pests won't go away. But the spray and swatter give you peace of mind. You know they will save your body from too many bites!

Like spraying or swatting away pesky bugs, God helps you get rid of lies that fly your way. Have you ever believed something about yourself that wasn't true? Did a friend say a hurtful word that was hard to forget? Negative thoughts can feel like nagging pests. They buzz around your head. It feels like they never leave you alone. But God has given you ways to chase away these negative thoughts.

When these thought pests come flying, seek God's Word. His truths found in the Bible will get rid of the swarming lies. Saying a verse out loud helps replace a lie with something true. Another way to swat a lie is to tell someone about it. They can help you find the truth. You can also put on spiritual bug repellant. Read the Bible each day to shield yourself with God's truth. Knowing what the Bible says will prevent future thought pests from landing on you.

So put on your bug spray. Take out your fly swatter. Start spraying away the lies with God's truth! God will give you peace of mind. No more buzzing, biting lies.

GOD'S PEACE will keep your HEARTS and MINDS.

~PHILIPPIANS 4:7~

GOD GIVES ME ENERGY

Yes, God is working in you to help you want to do what pleases him. Then he gives you the power to do it.

PHILIPPIANS 2:13

Windmills make electricity. The wind blows against giant blades that spin a generator. The faster the blades turn, the more electrical energy the windmill makes. Wires take the electricity from the windmill to a power center and then into buildings like your home. Your lights could be powered by the wind!

In the same way windmills make electricity, God gives you energy. His power inside of you sparks you to do His will. Is it hard to start your day sometimes? Are you struggling to find friends? Or maybe you need motivation to finish a long school assignment. Pray for God's power to help you. Tell Him you need more of His energy to do what pleases Him. God will be your power source.

God can give you power on the days you've lost your energy. He might remind you of a blessing to be thankful for so you can start your day with joy. He might show you a shared interest with someone in your class. Or He might help you learn something fascinating in your schoolwork. What task do you need some extra energy to tackle? Pray for God to get you moving.

God can power you through each day. Like a home powered by windmills, count on God for your energy. He will keep you spinning.

As you color, ask yourself where you need more of God's energy.
Tell God about the situation, and ask for His help.

GOD'S IDEAS FIT ME BEST

So we can say with confidence, "The Lord is my helper, so I will have no fear. What can mere people do to me?"

HEBREWS 13:6 NLT

How many balls can you juggle? Two? Maybe three if you've been working at it. Juggling takes a lot of practice! In fact, the world's best juggler started practicing when he was only four years old. And he dropped a lot of balls along the way. That's normal for a learning juggler! But he kept working at it, and he got better and better.

Have you ever felt like you were juggling different people's ideas about you? Mom expects you to get all A's. Grandpa wants you to join the football team. Your friends think you should play the video game that they like. These pressures can feel like juggling balls. You don't want to drop anything or be thought of poorly by others. And you don't want to disappoint anyone.

But it's okay to drop a ball that doesn't fit. One of the keys to juggling is to use the size of ball that's right for your hands. If someone's idea about you doesn't fit, let it go. Then ask God what to pick up in its place. Instead of making you good at football, God might give you a talent for making art on the computer. You can use your skill to make flyers for a church event or encourage someone with a picture. You might be more interested in making cookies than in playing that video game. But your friends won't mind if you make cookies while they play as long as you share with them!

God's ideas about you are the only ones that matter. Don't juggle expectations that don't fit just to please others. Pleasing God is all that matters. And His plans for you are always the right size!

GOD IS FAITHFUL

**"To the faithful you show yourself faithful; to those
with integrity you show integrity."**

2 SAMUEL 22:26 NLT

Did you know that most swans mate for life? A male swan and a female swan have a strong bond. Swans are known for their commitment to one another. They stay together until one dies. For this reason, the image of two swans stands for love. When swans bend their heads together, their necks form the shape of a heart. It is a display of their faithfulness toward one another!

Like swans stick by their mates, God will always be there for you. You are His, and He will be faithful, both now and forever. You have a special bond with Him that will last for eternity. Because God is completely committed to you, you can trust Him. He has the very best in mind for you. Jesus expressed His love for you by bending down from heaven to live on earth and die for you. The cross shows God's faithful love toward you. Because of Jesus' death on the cross, you can have a lifelong relationship with God. He will never leave your side!

Thank God for His faithfulness. Read His message in the Bible. Can you hear the love in His words? His faithful bond to you will never be broken.

I CAN HOLD TIGHTLY TO GOD

Let us hold tightly without wavering to the hope we affirm, for God can be trusted to keep his promise.

HEBREWS 10:23 NLT

Did you know that sea otters hold hands? Family members hold paws while they sleep. This keeps the otters from floating away from the group. Sometimes it's just one male otter and one female otter holding onto one another. Sometimes a whole family clings to each other. This is called a *raft* of otters. The group stays together no matter how strong the ocean current is. Staying together also keeps the otters safe from predators.

Like sea otters hold tightly to each other, you can cling to God. He wants you to stay close to Him! Grab onto God's Word. Reading Scripture keeps you from floating away from God and thinking about selfish or hurtful things. And no one can harm your soul when you're holding tightly onto God's truth. Worshiping God tightens your grip. You make your relationship with Him stronger when you spend time praising Him.

Hold tightly onto God like sea otters hold onto each other. He will keep you from floating away by doing things He doesn't want you to do. You're part of His family, and God doesn't want anyone leaving the group. No matter what life brings, or what strong currents come, stay close to Him for love and protection.

GOD IS BIGGER THAN MY TROUBLES

We have small troubles for a while now, but they are helping us gain an eternal glory. That glory is much greater than the troubles.

2 CORINTHIANS 4:17

One marble is very small. But imagine filling a bag with one hundred marbles. The bag would be heavy. The weight of one marble is nothing in comparison to a bag full of marbles!

No matter how many marbles you add to a bag or how many bags you pile together, God is bigger. It's the same way with your troubles. No matter how big or heavy your troubles are, the reward waiting for you is much bigger. God's glory, which you will see in heaven, outweighs all your troubles combined.

What's your perfect day? Baking chocolate chip cookies, watching movies, cuddling with your dog, and maybe playing with your neighbors? In all that fun, you would forget your troubles from the day before. You would forget the canceled trip, the lost game, or the fight. That's how heaven will be! Every day will be the best day ever, spent with your Maker. No sin. No lost games. And no canceled trips! The glory of God's goodness will be far greater than all the troubles of your whole life.

God will trade your bags of hard, heavy things for incredible blessings when you get to heaven. He will give you a new body and a beautiful place to live with Him. You will be perfect and holy. When trouble rolls toward you, remember the eternal glory that's waiting for you in heaven. Life's troubles will seem as light as a feather in comparison.

HIS GLORY IS GREATER.

I CAN GIVE MY DREAMS TO GOD

We can make our plans, but the LORD determines our steps.

PROVERBS 16:9 NLT

Imagine you're hiking up a trail with lots of steps. The trail runs along the edge of a steep mountain. There are many more steps before you get to the top. You look behind and see how far you've gone. One hundred steps at least! You tell yourself the view will be worth it. So you take another step up.

Like a beautiful mountain view, God has amazing things for you to see and experience. Do you have dreams of what you want to be when you're older? A firefighter? A teacher? Maybe a mad scientist! God cares about each of your dreams. Tell Him your hopes, and He will listen. Just don't hold your plans too tightly. God may not fulfill your dreams exactly as you want. He may have different steps for you. But His dreams for you are incredible.

Pray about your dreams. Tell God when they change. Tell Him when you're not even sure what you want. Trust Him to take you up the right steps. He will lead you to an even better view than you can imagine. And when you don't know what's ahead, thank God for where you already are. Look back and praise Him for the steps behind you. And look around. See what view is in front of you now!

Give God your dreams. Enjoy each step as you trust His plans. Let Him take you to the mountaintop. The view is sure to be stunning!

Think about your dreams for the future. Write each dream on a mountaintop. Give these dreams to God in prayer. Trust Him with wherever He is taking you, and thank Him for where you already are!

PROMISE 97

GOD KEEPS ME FRESH

Dear friends, we have these promises from God. So we should make ourselves pure—free from anything that makes body or soul unclean.

2 CORINTHIANS 7:1

How do you prepare a lemonade stand? Grab lots of fresh lemons. Squeeze out the juice. Be sure to remove all the seeds! Add some sugar. Then pour the pure lemonade into cups. It's ready to serve! Make sure to have a coin jar and a sign.

Like squeezing pure juice from a lemon, God keeps you pure. He makes you clean and fresh without any seeds of anger or pride. God purifies you through His Son Jesus, who died on the cross for all your sins. When you give your life to God, He forgives your sins once and for all. Then He continues to forgive new sins. He keeps removing seeds of sin from your heart so that you are one hundred percent His! God is always at His lemonade stand offering His fresh grace. And it doesn't cost a single penny!

Sometimes you can think ahead and do things to keep yourself pure. Planning ahead is a little like cleaning your countertop before you make lemonade. That will keep any bits of dirt or food out of the drink. Likewise, you can avoid anything that will spoil your body or soul. God might help you say words that only build people up. He might teach you to be more honest with your parents. These actions will keep you as pure and fresh as just-squeezed lemonade.

Ask God to purify you. He will remove every seed or speck of dirt from your heart. His grace is the sugar that will make your lemonade sweet. Each cup is refreshing.

I AM GOD'S ARTWORK

I praise you because you made me in an amazing and wonderful way.

PSALM 139:14

You stare at a blank sheet of paper. It stares back at you. Beside it, different colors of paint call to you. What will you paint? Will you sketch with a pencil first? You decide to splatter colors everywhere. It looks perfect! A colorful masterpiece.

God made you as His colorful masterpiece. You are His artwork, and He is so proud of what He created. Do you wish something was different about you? Maybe you wish for straighter hair or to be taller. It's hard wanting to be different. But God created you to be just the way you are. Like an artist at his canvas, God chose just the right colors and shapes to make you. You make the world more beautiful.

When an artist is painting, they step back from their canvas to get a better look. They squint their eyes. They might tilt their head. Then they add a few more details. God looks at you in the same way. Each detail of you means something to Him. Your hair, your height, and even your smile were purposefully painted by Him. He loves how He made you and is so proud of His art. It took a lot of work!

Thank God for making you as His masterpiece. You are a colorful and detailed work of art. He made you to be amazing and wonderful. And He doesn't make mistakes.

Draw a self-portrait inside the frame. Praise God for creating you just right.

I AM ON A MISSION FOR GOD

"For God loved the world so much that he gave his only Son. God gave his Son so that whoever believes in him may not be lost, but have eternal life."

JOHN 3:16

One of the greatest missions in US history was sending people to the moon. In 1969, NASA sent three brave astronauts to land on the moon. *Apollo 11's* crew included an astronaut named Neil Armstrong. He became the first human to step on the moon. As he waved at the TV camera attached to the landing module, the whole world celebrated.

Over two thousand years ago, God completed the greatest mission of all time. God sent Jesus to earth to pay for our sins. Anyone who believes in Him can live forever in heaven. It was a mission of great love!

God gives you a mission too. He tells you to share the Good News about forgiveness through Jesus to everyone in the world: Your family. Your friends at school. Your neighbors. Even your coach or babysitter!

Like the three astronauts on a mission together, you're on a mission with a crew of believers. Your church leader, your Christian friends, and everyone else who follows Jesus are part of that crew. Together, you can talk about God's love with others. Who do you know who needs to hear the Good News of Jesus? Ask God to show you the next step of your mission.

Fasten your helmet. Get the launch pad ready. It's time to broadcast God's mission of love. God made history when He sent Jesus. Help the world celebrate what He has done!

As you color, think about people you know who need to hear the Good News about Jesus and heaven. Ask God to help you complete your mission to them.

GOD SEALS ME WITH HIS HOLY SPIRIT

He put His mark on us to show that we are his. And he put his Spirit in our hearts to be a guarantee for all he has promised.

2 CORINTHIANS 1:22

Locks keep things secure. A lock will keep your bike safe when you park it at school. You can keep your favorite photos and special objects secret by storing them in a locked box. And a lock prevents pirates from opening a treasure chest of gold and jewels! Each lock has a key or combination. It's the only way to open the lock.

In the same way bikes and treasure chests are fastened with locks, you are secure in God. When you invite Jesus into your life, God locks your heart with His Holy Spirit. His presence will stay with you forever. God guarantees it! No one can take you away from God once you're His. Your security is being His child. And He promises you a forever home with Him in heaven!

God's promises to you will never change. There is no key to undo what He has done in your heart. His lock secures your life to Him. Nothing can take you away from God's family. You are His treasure, and He keeps you safe.

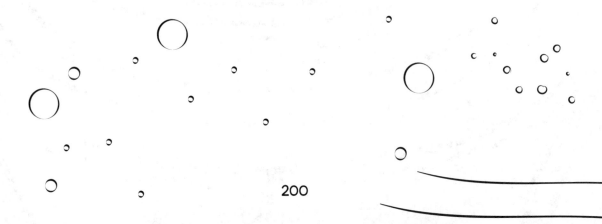

PACK YOUR WORRY SUITCASE

CRAFT FOR PROMISE 12: GOD CARRIES MY WORRIES

God wants to hold all your worries and challenges for you. Make a suitcase to pack away your concerns and let God take care of them.

Materials

small cardboard box or shoebox

colored paper

markers, crayons, or colored pencils

white paper

tape or glue

scissors

Directions

1. Cover the box with colored paper. Use as many colors as you like!

2. On the outside of your box, write words and sentences that remind you God will carry your worries, such as "God is my Helper" and "God knows what I need."

3. On white paper draw large shapes of clothing, supplies, and other items you'd pack for a trip. Color the items.

4. On each item, write a big challenge, goal, or worry you have.

5. Place the items in your box.

6. When you have a new worry, make another item for your box. Ask God to carry the worry for you.

After you've been using your worry suitcase for a while, open it and read your worries. Has God taken care of some of your old concerns?

SUNSHINE SIGN

CRAFT FOR PROMISE 70: I CAN FIND JOY IN GOD

Being thankful for our blessings fills our hearts with joy. Make this sunshine sign to help you have God's joy inside of you every day.

Materials

paper plate
markers
yellow and orange paper
scissors
glue or tape
popsicle stick

Directions

1. Color the paper plate yellow or orange on one side. Draw a smiling face.

2. Cut the paper into triangles of different sizes. You'll need about 15 triangles.

3. Write a blessing on each triangle.

4. Glue or tape the triangles around the edge of the plate on the side you didn't color. Be sure you can see the happy sun face and your blessings at the same time.

5. Tape or glue the sun onto a popsicle stick. Raise your sign high to praise God for all the blessings He has given you!

HOW TO MAKE AN ART PRAYER JOURNAL

Some people like to write down their prayers. Keeping a prayer journal makes it easy to look back and remember all the ways God has answered your prayers.

But you don't have to write your prayers. You can draw your prayers or use other kinds of art to talk to God. Make your own art prayer journal and get creative with your prayers.

Materials

small three-ring binder
copies of the prayer journal template
blank paper
three-hole punch
art supplies

Directions

1. Decorate the cover of the binder however you'd like. Make a collage, draw with markers, add stickers, or use your own creative idea. Don't forget to give your journal a title!

2. Copy the journal template on the opposite page to make the pages of your journal.

3. Mix in blank paper for more room to create.

4. Punch holes in all the pages with the three-hole punch. Insert the pages into the binder. Add more pages as you fill up your journal.

My Prayers

Date: _____

I praise God for: ♥

♥

Prayer for myself:

Prayer for my world:

Prayer for my family and friends:

Questions for God:

DRAW YOUR OWN BIBLE PROMISE #1

Read the Bible passage. Then draw a picture to illustrate the passage.

The Lord is my shepherd.
I have everything I need.
He gives me rest in green pastures.
He leads me to calm water.
He gives me new strength.
For the good of his name,
he leads me on paths that are right.

—PSALM 23:1–3

DRAW YOUR OWN BIBLE PROMISE #2

Read the Bible verse. Then draw a picture to illustrate the verse.

He will protect you like a bird spreading its wings over its young.

—PSALM 91:4

DRAW YOUR OWN BIBLE PROMISE #3

Read the Bible passage. Then draw a picture to illustrate the passage.

"I am the true vine; my Father is the gardener. . . . He trims and cleans every branch that produces fruit so that it will produce even more fruit. . . . I am the vine, and you are the branches. If a person remains in me and I remain in him, then he produces much fruit. But without me he can do nothing."

—JOHN 15:1–2, 5

AND MY GOD will supply EVERY NEED of yours ACCORDING to his riches in glory in CHRIST JESUS PHILIPPIANS 4:19